BREAKING THE RULES:
A Photo Media Cookbook

by Bea Nettles

Copyright© 1977 by Bea Nettles.
All rights reserved. No part of this book may be reproduced in any form or by any electronic or mechanical means, including information storage and retrieval systems without permission in writing from the publisher, except by a reviewer who may quote brief passages in a review.

First Edition

Published by Inky Press Productions, Rochester, N.Y.

Printed in the United States of America.

Library of Congress Cataloging in Publication Data

Nettles, Bea, 1946-
    Breaking the rules.
    Bibliography: p. 50
    1. Photography. 2. Photography—Apparatus
and supplies. I. Title.
TR350.N47   770'28   77-12930
  ISBN 0-930810-00-7

Exclusively distributed by: Light Impressions Corp., Box 3012, Rochester, NY 14614

Printing 10 9 8 7 6 5 4 3 2

INTRODUCTION

In the late 60's when I began to work with "non silver" materials, information and good examples were scarce. I was a painting graduate student with an interest in mixing processes including photography, printmaking, sculpture, drawing and painting.

My formal training in photography had been basic black and white printing. Other processes were learned slowly by watching, reading anything available, and asking questions. Often because I had no clear directions to follow or was not given a demonstration, I broke the rules. At best, exciting discoveries were made this way...at worst, time and effort produced no physical results. Such experimentation is one sure way to learn the limitations of materials and one's patience.

Luckily today, due to better communications, good distribution of publications, workshops, and teachers of these processes, there is widespread interest and information on such techniques as cyanotype, gum printing and the like.

The material in this handbook has been the basis of the workshops that I have given all over the USA for the past seven years. I keep an evergrowing notebook of processes and ideas and share them as I travel. Realizing that not everyone has a complete darkroom, I try to show ways that one can work with even the simplest equipment or occasional access to facilities.

Because I cannot give you actual demonstrations, I have tried to make the basic steps as clear as possible. In the book you will find comparisons of the processes and practical suggestions. I have also listed further reading, materials and products that you might find helpful. Some of the processes are covered in extensive detail in other guidebooks. I hope you will use this book and others as the basis for your own research. Make tests, find your own recipies, experiment, combine processes, push the limits...and try breaking the rules.

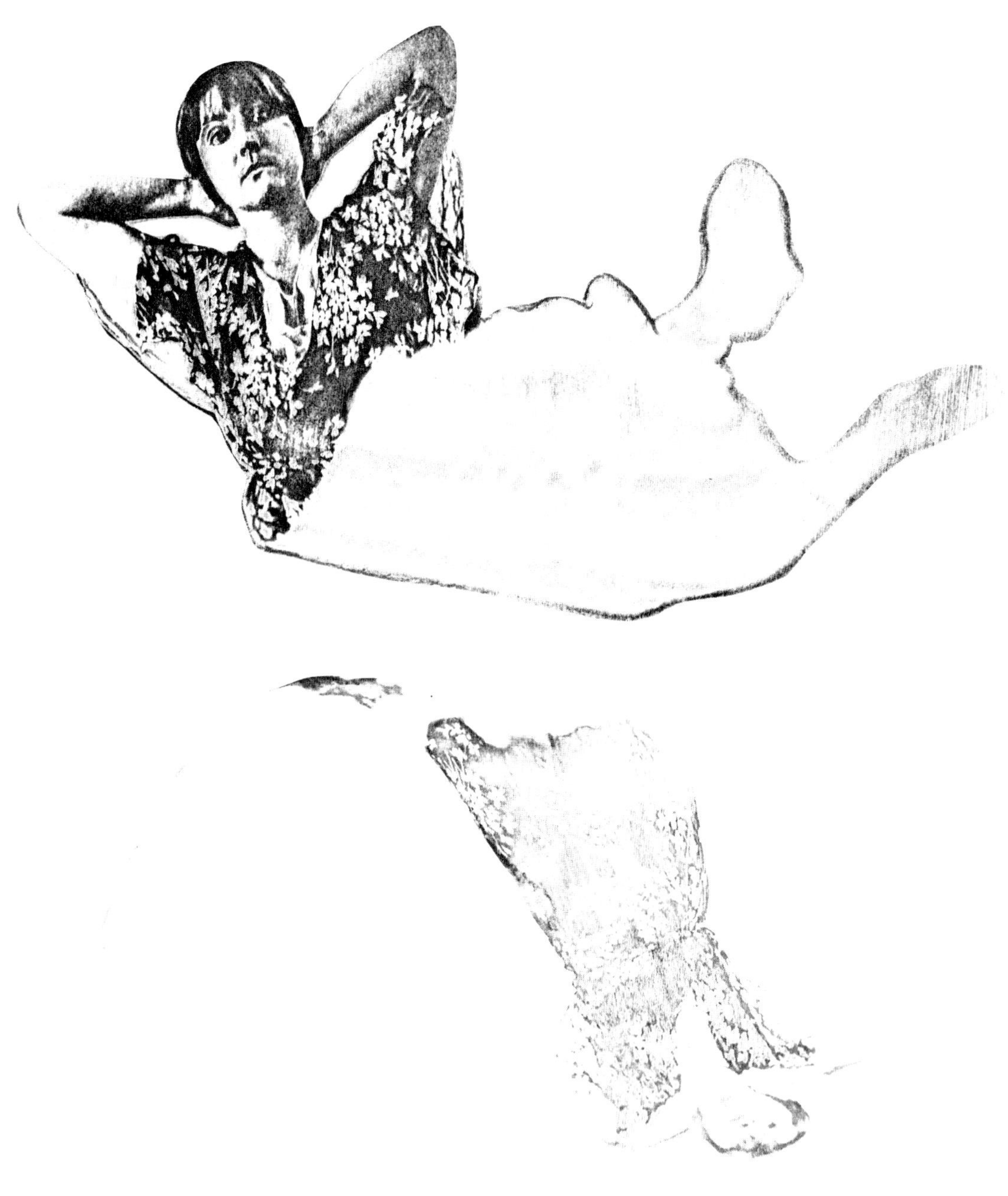

Page from "Dream Pages", Self Portrait produced by copying a photographic print with a Haloid Xerox machine, 1975.

CONTENTS

ALTERNATIVE PROCESSES: COMMERCIAL SOURCES

I always start my workshops with a sampling of commercial products available to anyone with the money to buy them and the ability to read the package directions. The products marked with a star (*) will be described in more detail later in the text, but in many cases all you need is to have the address and to know what the product is capable of. Write for catalogs and current price lists.

1. **Rockland Colloid Corporation**
    599 River Road
    Piermont, N.Y. 10968

Two of their products are listed below.

PRINT-E-MULSION CB 101

This is a black and white continuous tone emulsion that can be coated under safelight onto various surfaces including paper, cloth, wood, rocks, ceramics and tile. After the coating dries, the object is enlarged onto with a normal camera negative and developed in standard photographic paper chemicals. Very complete instructions are included with the emulsion.

Helpful Hints:
For warming the gelatin emulsion to liquid state, try immersing the container in an electric coffee pot full of hot water. This is much safer than taking a hot plate into your darkroom.

When coating the emulsion, keep everything very warm. Preheat the surface you're going to coat with a hair drier and keep the coating brush warm. This makes it easier to coat evenly. Then when processing the emulsion, keep the chemicals quite cool (65 degrees). This makes the emulsion less likely to lift off the surface.

PHOTO ALUMINUM
These sheets of aluminum are precoated with a continuous tone black and white emulsion. They are printed onto as if they were standard photo paper.

Helpful Hints:
To cut up the sheets in the darkroom, score them with a matte knife and snap them into sections.

Aluminum may be toned with photo toners.

2. **Luminos**
   25 Wolffe St.
   Yonkers, N.Y. 10705

PHOTO LINEN

White fabric that has been precoated with continuous tone emulsion. It is processed like photo paper and is available in standard sheets and rolls.

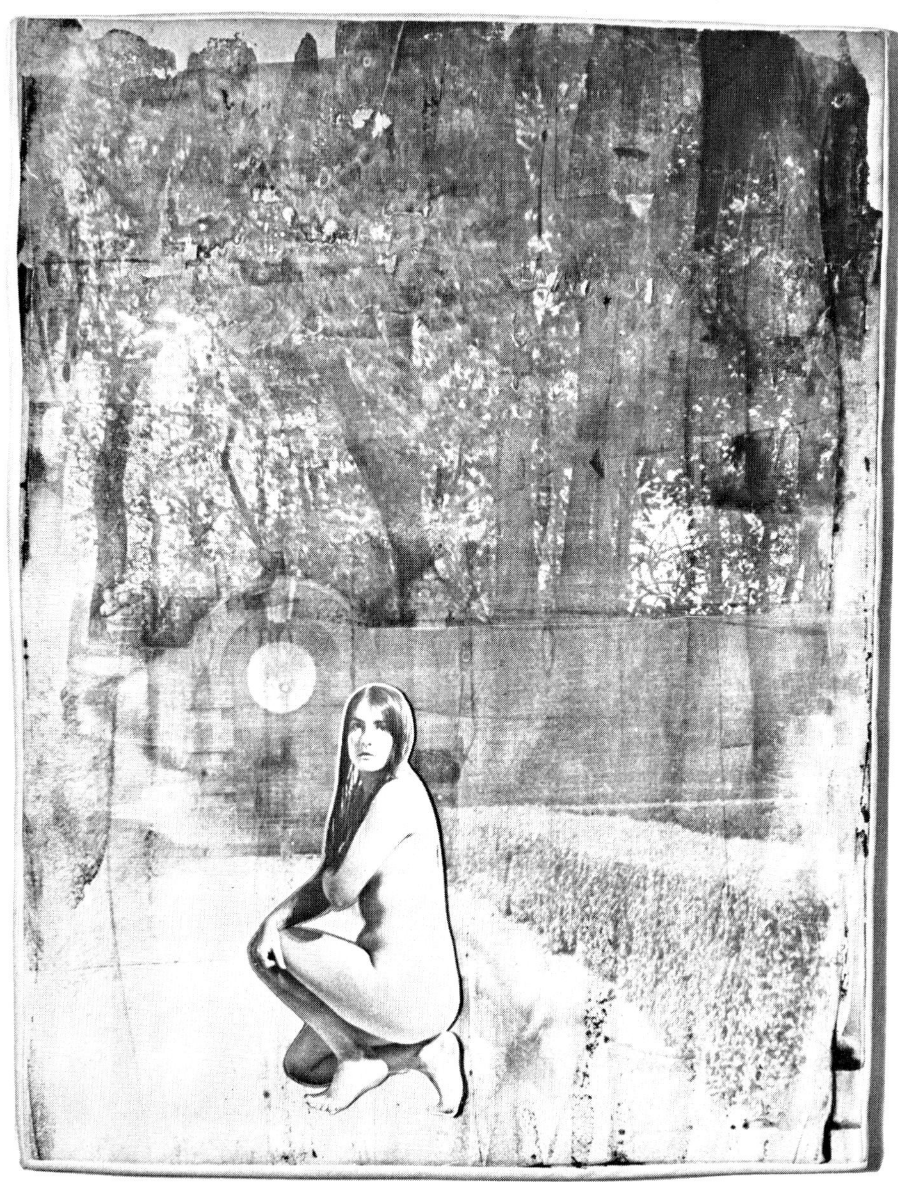

"Suzanna..surprised", Rockland Emulsion on cloth with Luminos Photo Linen figure. 28" x 36", 1970.

3. **Naz Dar Screen Process Products**
   1087 N. Branch Street
   Chicago, Ill. 60622

*NAZ DAR E—Z DIRECT METHOD PHOTO EMULSION
A light sensitive emulsion that is coated directly onto a stretched screen.

4. **Ulano Inc.**
   210 East 86th St.
   N.Y., N.Y. 10028

*ULANO PHOTO FILMS
Light sensitive films with gelatin coatings that are adhered to screens.

5. **Screen Process Supplies, Mfg. Co.**
   1199 East 12 St.
   Oakland, Ca. 94606

INKODYE
This is a permanent vat dye that is thick enough to be screen printed onto fabric. It may also be used for batik and tie dying of fabric. Imagery thus added to fabric is made permanent with heat or ultraviolet light.

GLASS ETCH
A thick paste that may be photo screen printed onto glass to lightly etch a frosted photographic image onto its surface.

6. **John Marshall Mfg. Co.**
   167 N. 9th St.
   Brooklyn, N.Y. 11211

*PHOTO RETOUCH COLORS
Sets of concentrated water based color for retouching color photographs. Useful for hand coloring black and white photographic emulsions such as photo paper, photo linen, photo aluminum, and ortho film.

*PHOTO OIL PENCILS
These are oil paint in pencil form for hand coloring photographs. Oil color is the most permanent method of hand coloring photos.

7. **Edwal Scientific Products**
    12120 S. Peoria St.
    Chicago, Ill. 60643

*PHOTO TONERS
These toners are available in 5 colors (red, blue, yellow, green, brownish-orange). They convert the greys in photographic emulsions to colors leaving the whites clear. Useful on all silver based materials including Rockland Emulsion, Photo Linen, Photo Aluminum and ortho film. The results will not meet archival standards.

8. **3M Company, Printing Products Division**
    3M Center
    St. Paul, Minn. 55101

3M COLOR KEY
This clear film with a color base may be contact printed through a halftone or a high contrast film image with a bright light source. It is then developed with 3M Developer and a cotton pad yielding a crisp photographic image in the color of your choice on a clear acetate backing. Color Key is available in negative and positive acting sheets, opaque or transparent, in a wide range of colors. Sizes range from 8½" x 11" to 20" x 24". It is expensive and the results are not permanent. It is primarily used as a proofing method.

9. **Light Impressions Corporation**
    Framing Division
    131 Gould Street
    Rochester, N.Y. 14610
    716-271-8960

Write for an extensive catalog of archival framing supplies, unusual chemicals, and artists' papers.

*KWIK PRINT
Sensitized Kwik Print colors are applied with cotton pads onto specially prepared vinyl sheets, contact printed through large negatives and developed by washing in water. These colors may also be used on artist's paper and cloth. They are permanent and washable.

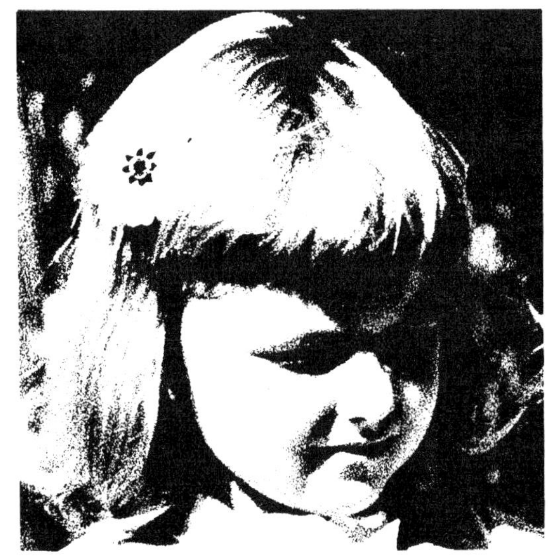

*Enlargement of HIGH CONTRAST
IMAGE (page 9)*

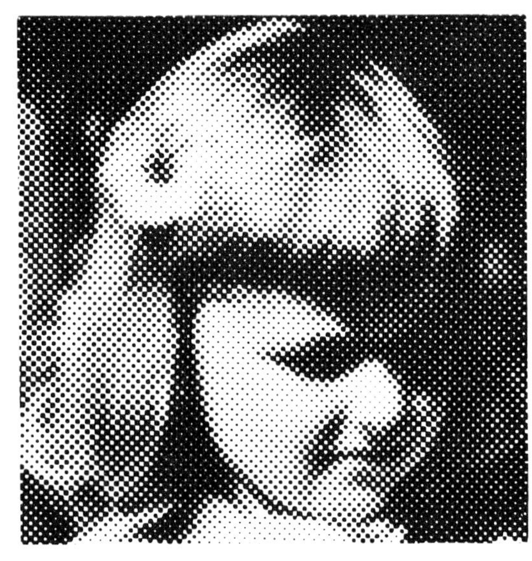

*Enlargement of HALFTONE DOT
IMAGE (page 12)*

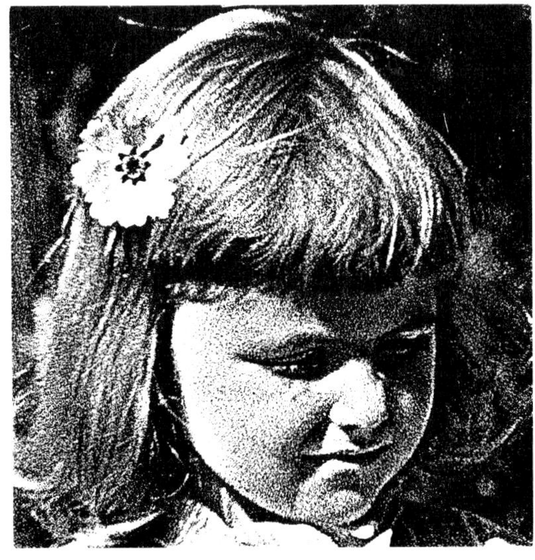

*Enlargement of RANDOM DOT
IMAGE (page 18)*

GRAPHIC ARTS FILMS

Large contact size film images are used in the processes listed below. Several types of film are described which can be used to achieve four basic results:

HIGH CONTRAST — An image composed of only black and clear areas. Printers refer to these images as "line shots."

HALFTONE DOT — An image composed of only black and clear dots of varying sizes arranged on a checkerboard grid. They give the illusion of continuous tone and are commonly used in newspapers and books. "Moire" patterns often occur when 2 halftones are overlapped to form plaids.

RANDOM DOT — An image composed of only black and clear areas arranged in randomly spaced grainy dots.

CONTINUOUS TONE — An image composed of black, grey, and clear areas. (Because offset printing cannot yield true continuous tone, no examples can be included in this text).

For Positive image use a:	*High Contrast results*	*Halftone or Random Dot results*	*Continuous Tone Results*
Cyanotype	negative	yes	yes	yes
Van Dyke Brown	negative	yes	yes	yes
Kwik Print	negative	yes	yes	yes
Gum Print	negative	yes	yes	difficult
Offset Lithography	negative	yes	yes	no
Screen Printing	positive	yes	yes *(if screen is fine enough)*	no
Photo Etching	positive	yes	yes	no

BASIC DARKROOM SETUP FOR ORTHO FILM

Purchase Kodalith A-B Developer from a Graphic Arts Supply and mix according to directions.

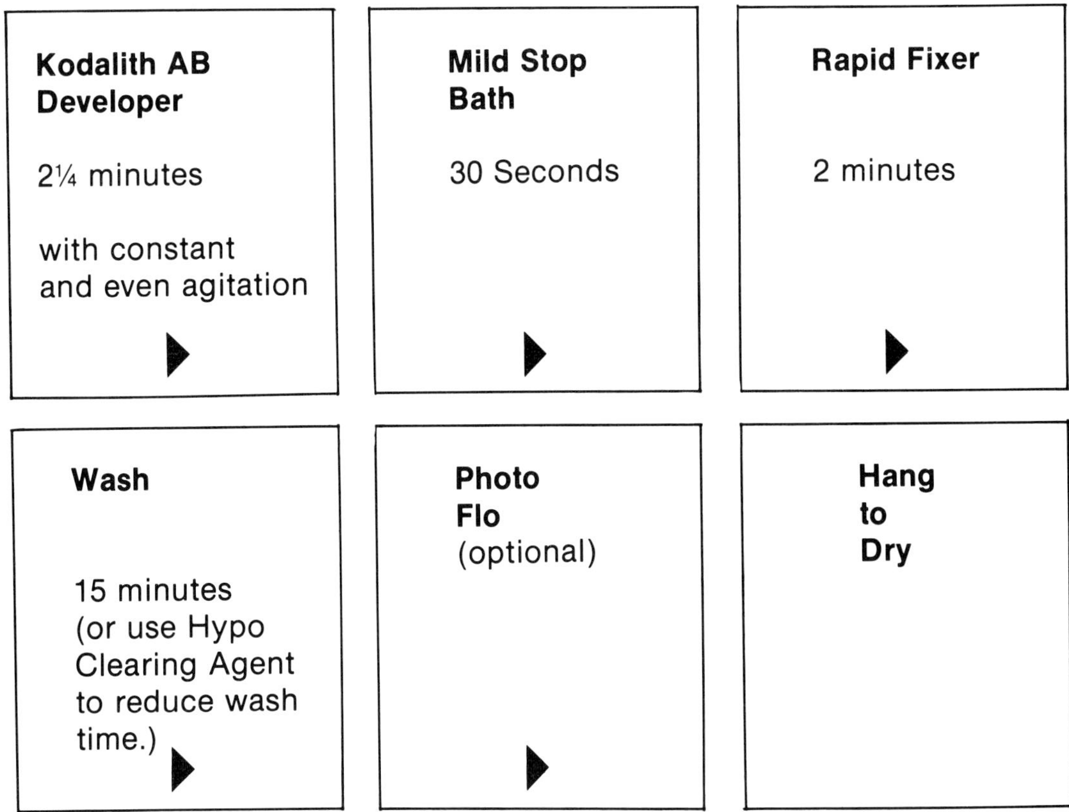

For processing, follow directions packed with the film. Basically most graphic arts films use the above sequence of chemicals. Although most directions state that you must use a red safelight, I often use a yellow OC filter at least 6 feet away from the film and developer with no noticeable effects.

Expose the ortho film with a negative in the enlarger as you would photographic paper. Place milky side of the film up (although you can also expose through the backing side).

ALWAYS MAKE A TEST STRIP! That is, cut a small strip of film and give it a range of exposures and develop it using these basic processing directions.

BASIC TYPES OF GRAPHIC ARTS FILMS

There are many types of graphic arts films that may be handled under safelight in a darkroom.
Those listed below are available in standard sheet sizes and often in rolls from Graphic Arts Supply Stores.

Brand Name	Description	Advantages	Disadvantages
Kodak Kodalith Ortho Film Type 3 **Agfa Gevaline Ortho Ilfolith**	Depending on the developer these films will yield high contrast or continuous tone results. Kodalith will yield random dots with special development in Kodak Fine Line.	Versatility Readily available in many sizes.	
Kodak Fine Grain Positive Film Type 7302	This is a continuous tone film developed in Dektol (1:2) under normal yellow safelight.	Cheaper than ortho film	Continuous tone results only. Largest size is 11" x 14".
Kodak High Speed Duplicating Film Type 2575	This film gives a continuous tone negative image when a negative is enlarged or contact printed onto it.	One step process. Speed.	More expensive than ortho film.
Kodak Autoscreen Ortho Film	Yields 133 line halftone images	Eliminates need for halftone screens.	Expensive. Not recommended for processes requiring multiple exposures because moire patterns often result.
Kodak Translite Film 5561	This film has a thick frosted base with the appearance of tracing paper.	Useful for drawing or hand coloring.	Usually a special order item.

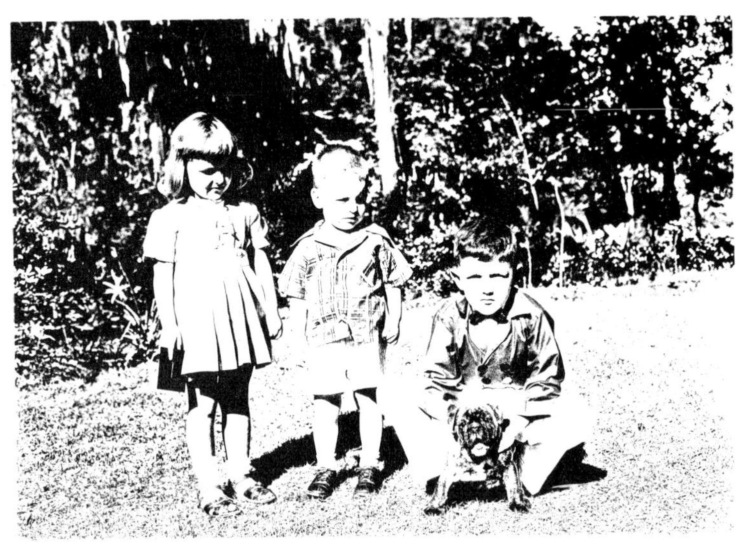

High contrast example.

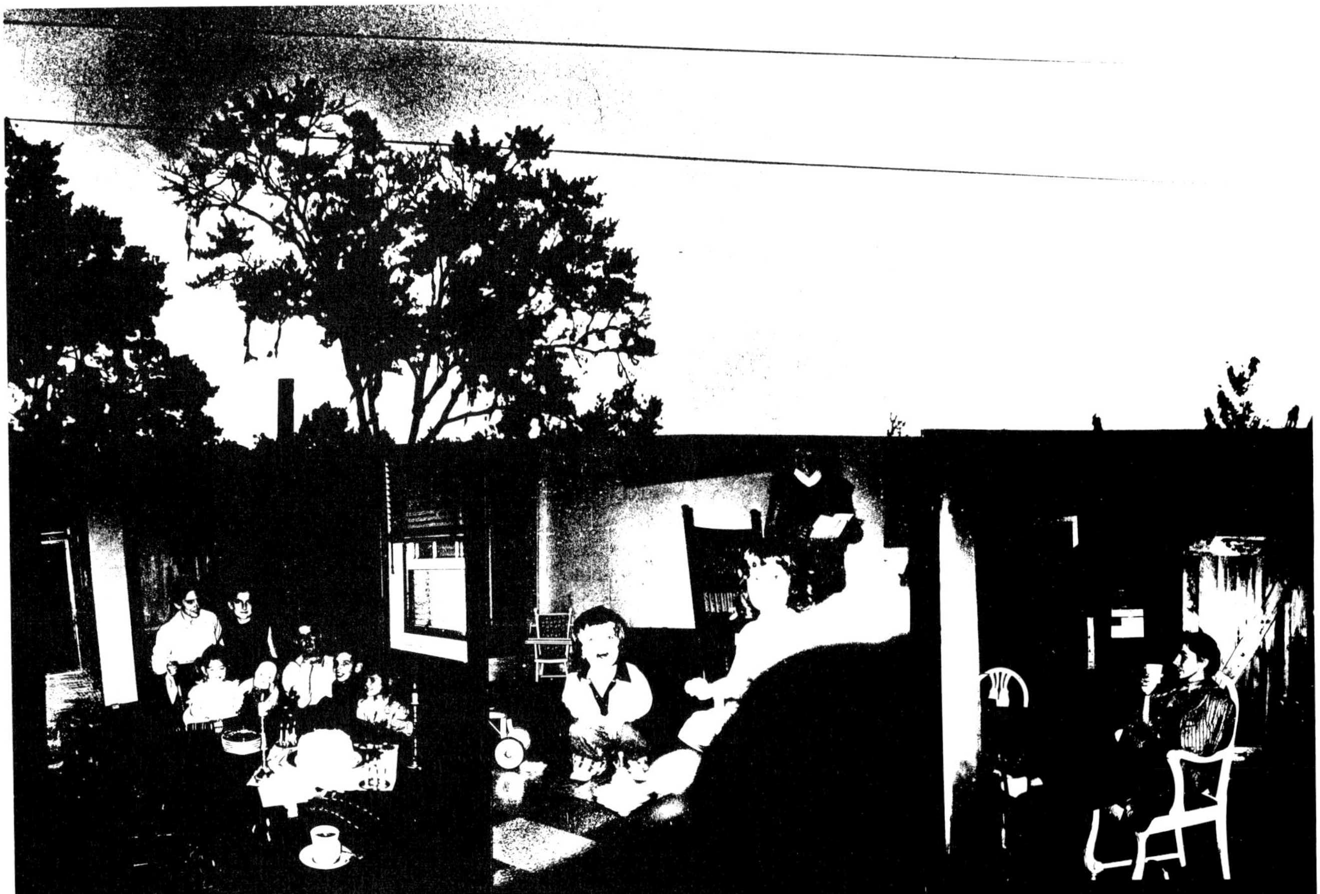

High contrast page from "The Elsewhere Bird", 1974.

HOW TO USE ORTHO FILM

1. To make a HIGH CONTRAST POSITIVE

Use basic darkroom setup.
    Enlarge a negative directly onto ortho film and process in AB Developer for 2¼ minutes. Do a test strip and don't play with the development time, as the image can change drastically in the last few seconds of development.

2. To make a CONTINUOUS TONE POSITIVE

    Enlarge negative as above, but process it in Dektol mixed 1 part to 6 parts water for 1½ minutes. For this process ortho film is usually overexposed and underdeveloped.

3. To make a HIGH CONTRAST NEGATIVE (with AB Developer; see 1 above)
    or CONTINUOUS TONE NEGATIVE (with Dektol; see 2 above), *either:*

    Contact print a positive ortho film image onto a 2nd piece of ortho film.
    Contact print a single weight paper print (emulsion side down), drawing or magazine image onto ortho film.
    Enlarge a small film positive made by contact printing a camera negative onto a small piece of ortho film, or slightly enlarging a 35mm negative to a 4 x 5" positive. This is the crudest method, but it's cheap.
    Enlarge a positive black and white or color slide onto ortho film.
    Expose ortho film in a pinhole or view camera, or expose a roll of 35mm ortho film.
    Expose ortho film through photogram material (lace, leaves, rice, Ajax, grits, gummed stars, fabric, etc.)

HOW TO USE DUPLICATING FILM

1. To make a CONTINUOUS TONE NEGATIVE

Use basic darkroom setup.
   Place a normal negative in your enlarger and enlarge it onto a test strip of high speed duplicating film.
   Develop the film for 2¼ minutes following basic darkroom setup and you will get a continuous tone **negative** from your **negative.**
   Remember the duplicating film has been pre-exposed and the longer you expose it, the lighter it will get. If the developing image is **too dark** you need **more exposure.**

   This film is a marvelous time saver as it gives you copy negatives with one step. You must learn to think in reverse which can drive you crazy when you dodge and burn:

> Dodging makes the image area darker.
> Burning makes the image area lighter.

2. To make a HIGH CONTRAST or GRAINY NEGATIVE

Use basic darkroom setup.
   Because you will get a copy of your camera negative:
      Use a grainy negative (Tri X or Recording film) for grain.
      Use a high contrast negative (Ortho) for high contrast.

3. To copy GLASS PLATE NEGATIVES

Use basic darkroom set-up.
   Contact print old negatives or glass plates onto this film for use with alternative processes.

HOW TO USE AUTOSCREEN ORTHO FILM

Autoscreen is a versatile ortho film with a built-in 133 line dot pattern. Directions are enclosed with the film and a more detailed pamphlet is listed in the Helpful Reading section.

1. To make a HALFTONE POSITIVE
Use basic darkroom setup. It is important to use Kodalith Developer. Enlarge a camera negative onto Autoscreen and process it as you would ortho film. Because of its "built-in" dot pattern, the result is a halftone positive.

Check the dots with a magnifying lens. Ideally there should be small (10%) open dots in the shadow areas. This is critical if you plan to do photo etching and desirable if you plan to use this positive to make negatives for offset printing. If you plan to do either of these processes, by all means refer to Kodak Pamphlet #P21.

2. To make a HALFTONE NEGATIVE
Either:
Contact print an Autoscreen halftone positive onto plain ortho film and process using the basic darkroom setup;
Or:
Expose Autoscreen in your pinhole or view camera. Its ASA is 3½, so you will need 1-5 minute exposures. Process these negatives by inspection, in other words develop them until they look good, preferably with detail in the shadow areas. (See Pinhole Camera Section).

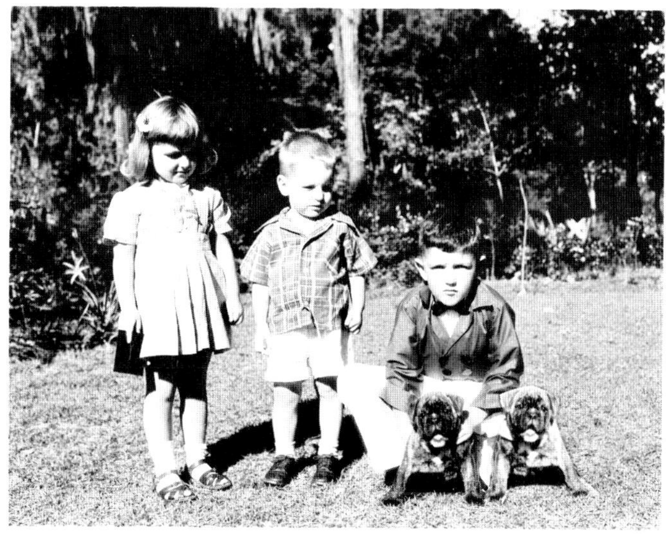

"D is for Double Dogs", 133 line halftone image from
A IS FOR APPLEBITING ALLIGATORS, 1974.

HOW TO USE HALFTONE SCREENS AND ORTHO FILM IN A DARKROOM

A halftone screen is an investment and with care it can be reused for years. The screen will be expensive and it is recommended for purchase only if you plan to do serious screen printing, offset printing, or photo etching. Screens come in various dimensions (11 x 14, 16 x 20, etc.) and in different dot sizes from coarse (45 line) through very fine (300 line) screens. Sometimes you can buy slightly scratched, second hand ones from printers.

1.   To make a HALFTONE POSITIVE
Use basic darkroom setup with Kodalith Developer.
   Lay the halftone screen on top of a test piece of ortho film in a contact printer (or put a piece of glass on top of the screen to hold it in contact).
   Expose your camera negative through the halftone screen onto the ortho film. Longer exposures are required because of the density of the halftone screen.
   After processing the ortho film test strip, inspect it with a magnifying lens. Choose the exposure time that yields satisfactory detail.

2. To make a HALFTONE NEGATIVE
Either:
Contact print a halftone positive made following step 1 onto plain ortho film
Or:
Project a normal negative through a halftone screen that has been placed in contact with Duplicating Film.

Take care of your screen and always replace it in its folder immediately after each use. It may be cleaned with film cleaner and lens tissue if necessary. You may wish to put a small piece of tape on one corner so that you can easily tell which is the top side of the screen (usually the brand name is written on the side that should be placed towards the light source).

WHAT A PROCESS CAMERA CAN DO FOR YOU

The most direct and professional way to make large negatives from positive imagery (photos, type, etc.) is to use a process or "copy" camera. The problem is of course, to gain access to one. They are used by the graphic arts industry and are sometimes found in university graphic arts departments. If someone will demonstrate its use to you, the process camera can save you time and enable you to do some very interesting things. If you cannot actually use one yourself, you can pay to have a printer do some work for you. First, let's assume you've decided to become a paying customer.

HOW TO COMMUNICATE WITH A CAMERAMAN

A good cameraman (or camerawoman) can work miracles, but it helps to know his limitations and what you want to have done.

1. *What size negative do you want?*

If the cameraman makes an exact copy negative of your positive original he will shoot it at 100%. He can also make a negative that is half the size of the original by shooting it at 50%, or slightly larger at 125%, and so on. The larger the negative, the more it is going to cost you. It is a good idea to stay close to standard film sizes because he usually has a price for 4 x 5, 5 x 7, 8 x 10 and you will often be charged for the entire piece of film (example a 6 x 9 negative will cost you the 8 x 10 price).

2. *Do you want a line shot (high contrast) or halftone?*

LINE shots are used primarily for type, line drawings and charts. No halftone screen is used and the negative is a high contrast copy of your original positive artwork. This is the cheapest method, if it suits your imagery. If the image already has a halftone dot, i.e. magazine image, a line shot is usually fine.
HALFTONE negatives are generally made from continuous tone imagery such as photographs and painted illustrations. You should specify what size dot screen you would like to have used. Most printers use 133-150 line screens unless you specify otherwise.

3. *Do you want increased contrast, lowered contrast, or an exact copy of your original?*

If you're having a halftone negative made from one of your photographs, the cameraman should be able to reproduce the tones faithfully if he uses the controls available to him. The main control is referred to as the "flash" exposure which pre-exposes the film through the halftone screen and gives control over the contrast of the resultant negative.

If your original print is rather flat and you would like increased contrast, you can request that he give the halftone a "bump" exposure. This increases the highlights by filling them in somewhat. Flashing and bumping in the darkroom sounds rather strange at first, but it's part of the vocabulary.

4. *Do you want a duotone made?*

Many fine books are printed in duotone. From one original artwork, two different halftone negatives are made. One halftone is shot for the highlight detail and the other contains the shadow detail. The negatives are printed one over the other and the richest possible tonal range is achieved. This is expensive because two negatives must be made with the halftone dots at angles to each other to avoid moire.

5. *Do you want color separation negatives?*

This is going to be very expensive, because it's complicated. Working from a color original, the cameraman makes 4 different halftone negatives using a different color filter over his camera lens each time. The halftone screen is rotated at specific angles for each of the 4 negatives so that when the 4 are printed together there will be no moire pattern. You can take these 4 color separation negatives and print them in a variety of techniques using cyan (blue), magenta, yellow and black to reconstruct your original image. This may be done with offset lithography, Kwik Print, Color Key, photo etching, screen printing and gum printing.

6. *How to judge the results.*

Ask to see the negative and look closely at it on a light table.

A line shot should be crisp, in focus, and any dust marks or pinholes should be opaqued (painted out).

A halftone should be inspected with a magnifying glass. I always carry one with me, which impresses a cameraman immediately. The dot pattern should be evenly developed with no hot spots, streaks, or dust spots. In the open areas which will print as black, there should be 10% black dots. This is especially important if the image is to be printed in ink because a solid black tends to be slow drying (and in offset printing the ink from one sheet tends to "set off" or stick to the back of the sheet stacked on top of it).

You can ask to see a proof of the negative which should give you an idea of its tonal range compared to the original. It is not unusual to request that something be reshot if the minimum standards listed above are not met.

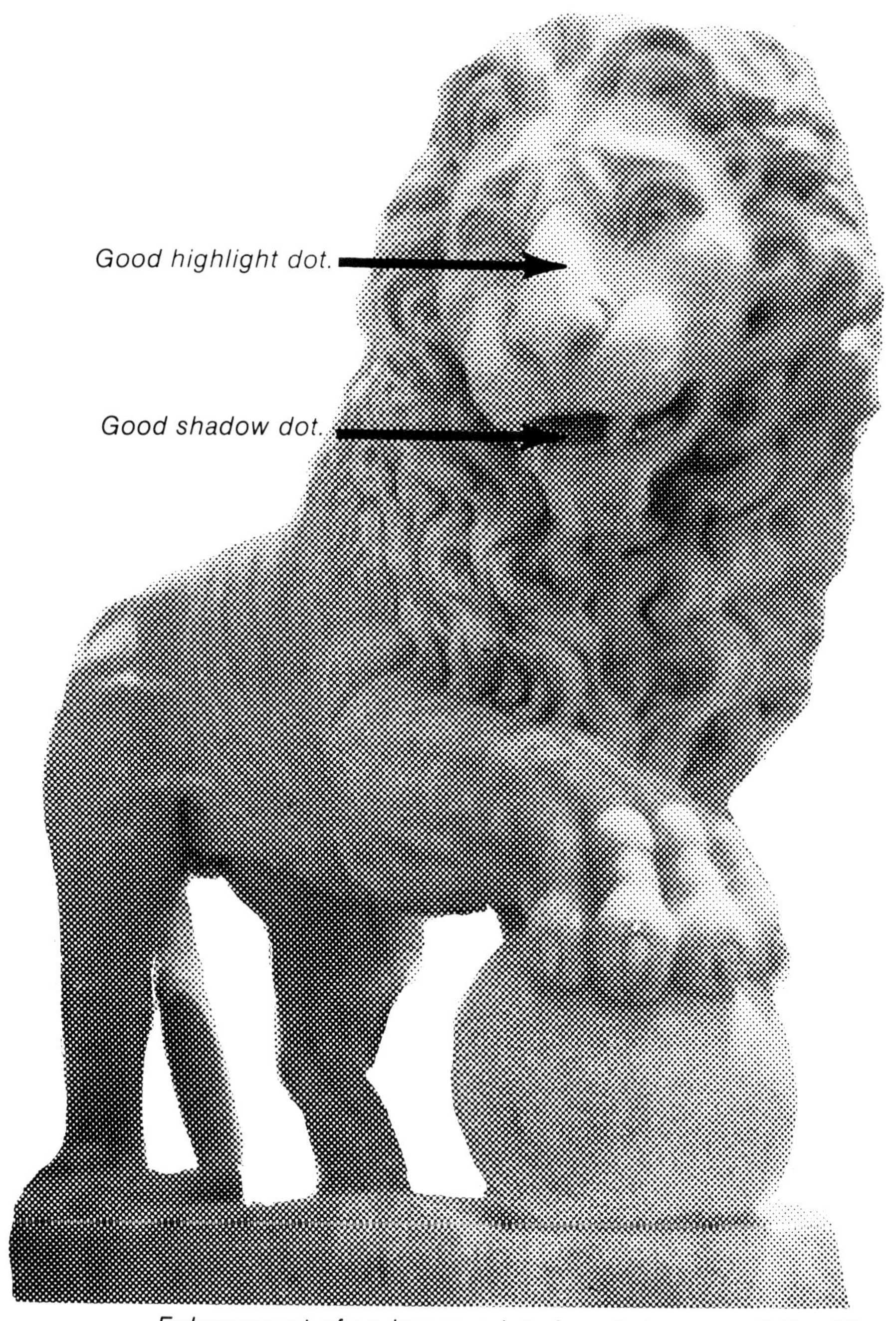

Enlargement of an image printed on Autoscreen Ortho Film.

HOW TO BECOME YOUR OWN CAMERAMAN

Process cameras are very expensive pieces of equipment. If you can gain access to one be sure to have a complete demonstration from a qualified operator. If this is not possible, read the manual for that particular camera or buy a generalized one.

Using the process camera you can produce from positive imagery:
High Contrast negatives
Halftone negatives (using either a halftone screen or Autoscreen)
Continuous tone negatives (using Dektol Developer 1/6)
Random Dot negatives (see directions in this book)

Some of the main advantages of the process camera are:

Ability to **copy and alter scale** of existing imagery (i.e. found objects, photos)
Ability to **copy flat objects,** (printed fabric, lace, leaves)
Unification of collages or drawing with mixed media into one surface on a single negative.

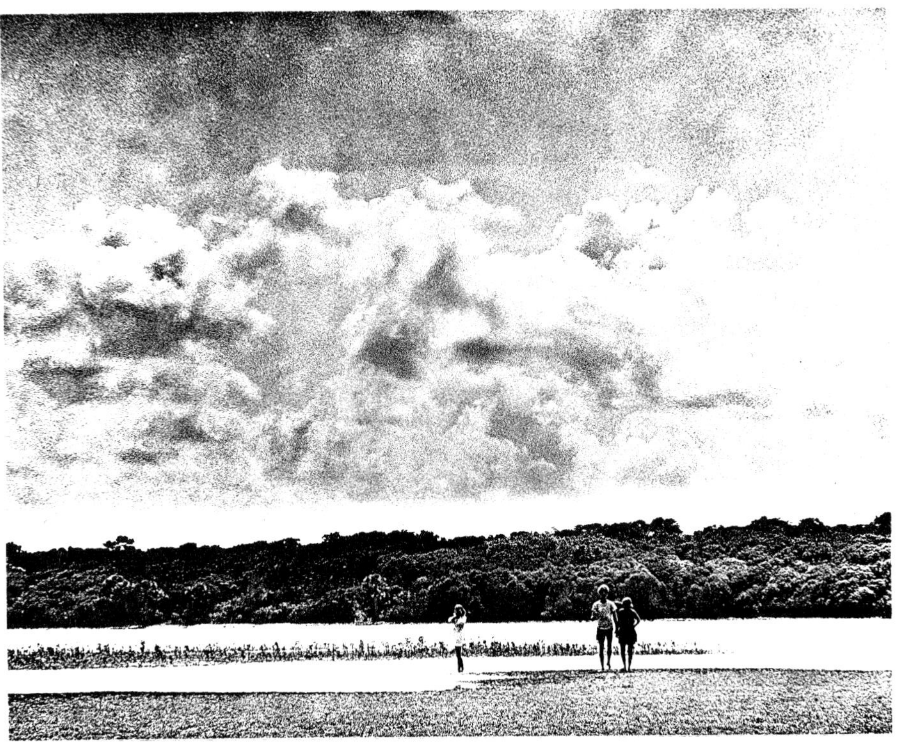

Example of a random dot image.

RANDOM DOT IMAGES ON ORTHO FILM

With special technique, Kodalith Ortho Film can be processed to yield random dot images. These images are made up of tiny black grains of a variety of shapes and sizes. The results are as fine as a 100 line halftone screen. The process has several advantages:

Random dot negatives don't form moire patterns when superimposed.
No need for halftone screens or Autoscreen.

Random dot images may be used for all processes described in this book as well as offset lithography and photoetching.

To make a *RANDOM DOT POSITIVE*
Use basic darkroom setup *except* for the developer.
   Mix KODALITH *FINE LINE* AB DEVELOPER according to the directions. This developer must be at 70 degrees and mixed fresh every 30 minutes or every few sheets of film!
   Enlarge a grainy camera negative (preferably Tri-X or Recording Film) onto a sheet of Kodalith Ortho Film Type 3 (it must be Kodak's Kodalith).

Develop this sheet in the Fine Line Developer:
        Agitate 15 seconds only.
        Let film sit still in tray for 2 minutes.
        (Tray must have a flat bottom, no ridges)

Follow basic steps from here on.

Result: A random dot positive which may be enlarged or contact printed onto ortho film to make a negative.

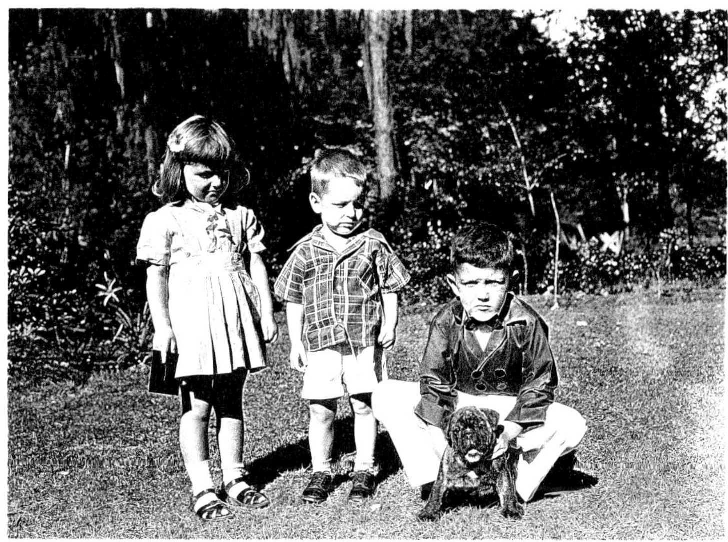

Example of a random dot image.

PINHOLE CAMERAS AND ORTHO FILMS

One of the most direct ways to make large ortho negatives is to build your own pinhole camera. Ortho film can be loaded directly into it, exposed, and developed in a simple darkened room. Very exciting results can be obtained in minutes. Of course, if you have a view camera, it can also be used to expose ortho film.

THE CAMERA

Choose a light tight box or construct one with chipboard and black photo tape. Spray the inside with flat black spray paint. Keep the outside a light color, as a dark color will absorb a lot of light and overheat the camera and the film.

A 4 x 5 wide angle camera can be made from an oatmeal or grits box.

An 8 x 10" wide angle camera can be made from a 5 gallon circular ice cream container.

A panoramic camera can be made by placing several pinholes in a circular ice cream container. (A three dimensional object coated with Rockland Emulsion can be exposed in such a camera).

THE PINHOLE

This is the most important part. Choose a fine needle and some metal foil, like an aluminum pie pan. Push the needle into the foil to make a dimple, reverse foil and sand the dimple with fine sandpaper until the hole opens up. Continue to push the needle into the hole, twirling it around and sanding, and checking with a magnifying glass until you make a perfectly round clear pinhole with no ridges.

Spray the back of the foil with black paint and tape it in place on the front of your camera. Black photo tape will serve as a lens cap and shutter.

THE FILM AND DEVELOPMENT

Any ortho film will work. The speeds may vary with the brand from about 2-5 ASA. You can also use Autoscreen (ASA 3½) or Fine Grain Positive Film 7302. Follow directions for processing each film as discussed earlier in this book. You can develop either high contrast or continuous tone negatives depending on the developer that you use. Continuous tone negatives can be developed by inspection in Dektol 1:6 for about 1 minute. Other types of negatives should be developed by inspection from 2-5 minutes.

EXPOSURES

Depending on the size of your pinhole, exposures range from 2-10 minutes outside. Compensate accordingly if the sun goes under a cloud. There's a lot of room for error here and you will soon know what your pinhole camera is capable of.

Why not try some deliberate double exposures or move objects around during the long exposures? Try a multiple pinhole camera...have fun!

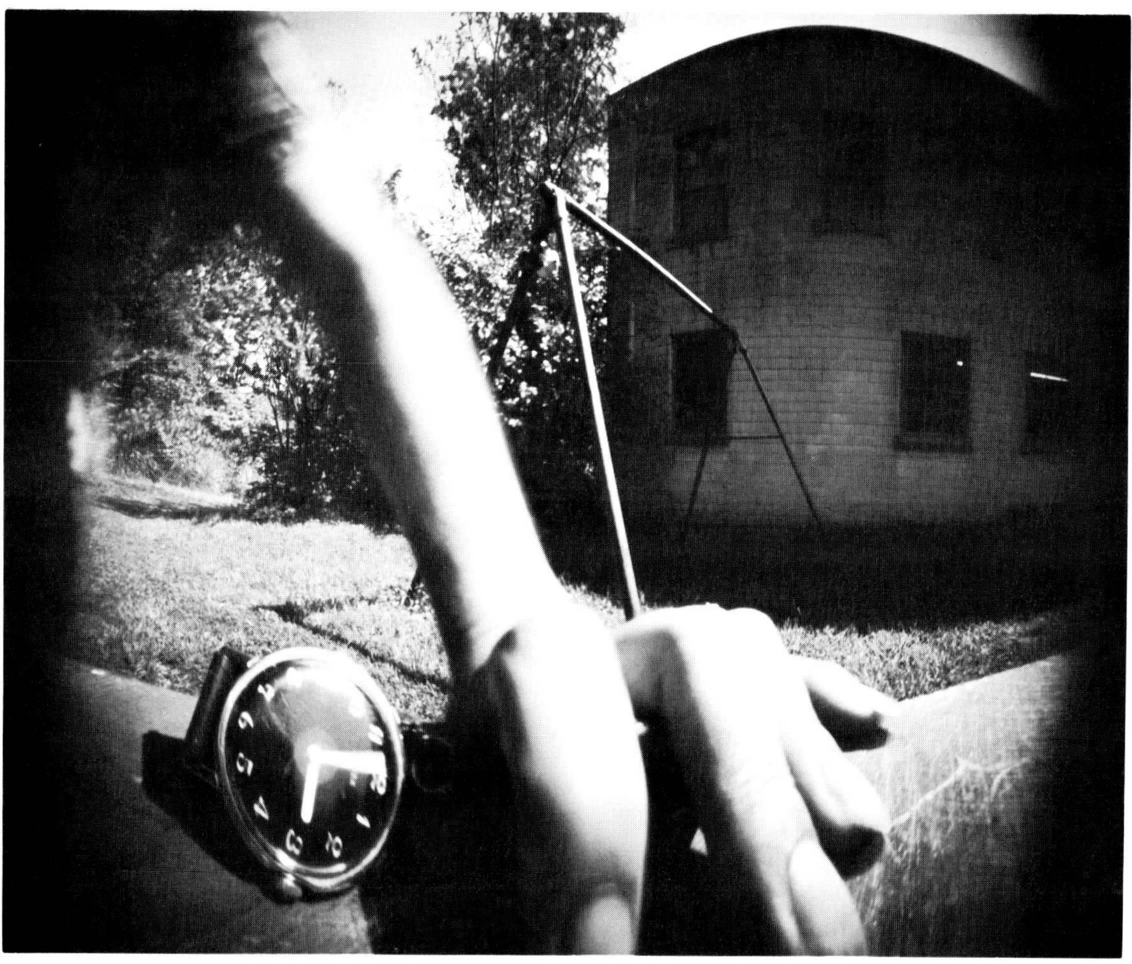

A 5 x 7 Autoscreen negative made in a grits pinhole camera. You can see that the exposure time was about 3 minutes.

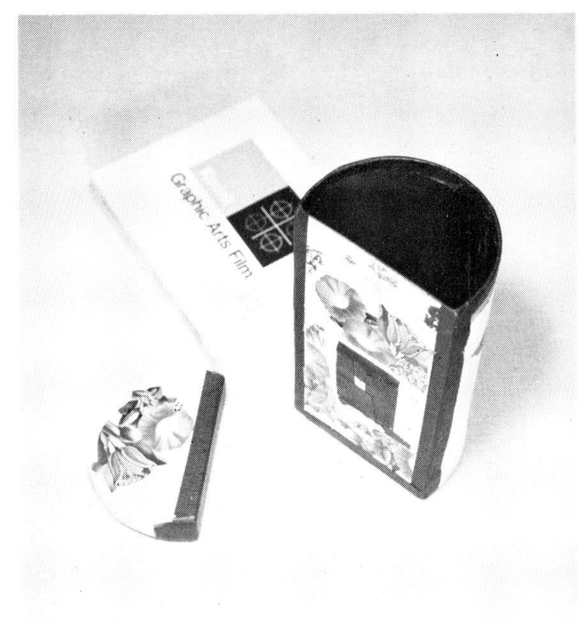

A grits box 4 x 5 camera.

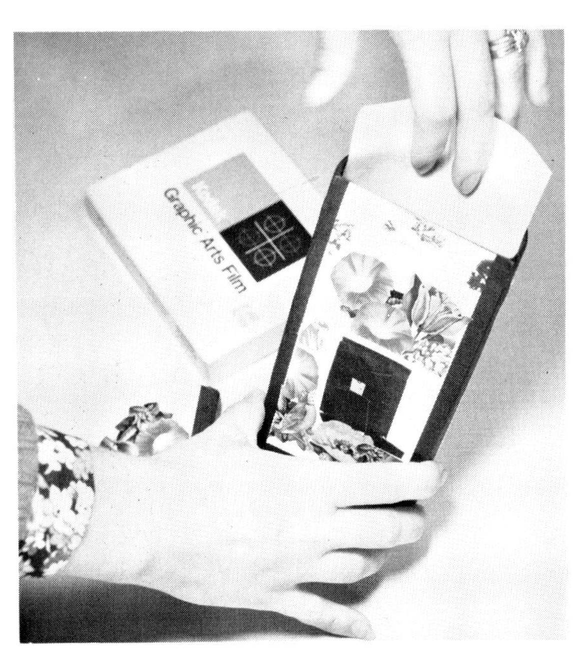

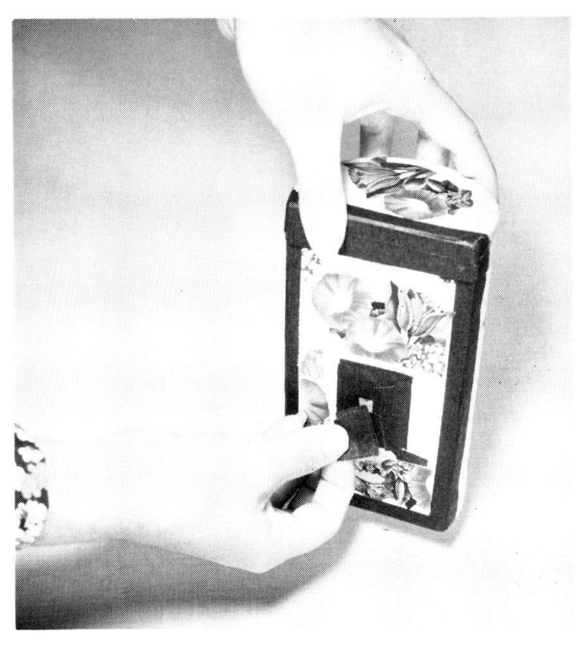

XEROGRAPHY

In increasing numbers, artists are gaining access to advanced quick copy machinery including black and white processes like Xerox and the Graphic Sciences Teleprinter, and color processes like the Color Xerox and the 3M Color-in-Color Machine. There are a few places in the USA that incorporate the use of such machines in Generative Systems programs. Even the simplest of these machines offers an image maker certain opportunities.

BLACK AND WHITE COPY MACHINES

Perhaps you can locate a machine operator who will let you supply your own artist's paper to load into such a machine. If so, you can "xerox" anything onto that surface. You can then take this image and apply blue print, brown print, Kwik Print, pencil, magazine rubbing, etc. on the surface.

COLOR COPY MACHINES

These machines are now located in many cities. Ask the operator to show you several things these machines can do including:
Full color copy of your original artwork on paper (some operators will let you use any paper you wish)
Full color copy of a projected 35mm slide.
Full color copy on acetate.
Full color copy on heat transfer material which can be ironed onto cloth.

By experimenting you will find ways to use black and white and color images:

1. Transfer of Machine Images
This works very much like the magazine rubbing method described in the next section. A good solvent is paint remover. Place the image face down on a smooth paper or cloth surface. Brush paint remover over the back of the image and rub gently with a spoon. This requires skill and timing. In this way you can make large scale composite artwork.

2. Flexible Machine Image Lifts
Read the section describing magazine lifts in this book. Ask the machine operator to install clay coated paper in the machine. After the copy is made you can coat its surface with gloss acrylic medium and make a lift of it.

MAGAZINE RUBBINGS

There are several ways that the ink from the printed page can be transferred to paper or cloth.

1. Select magazine image

Anything printed on newsprint or clay coated magazine paper (like the paper in Time, etc.) will transfer. Avoid images that have been heavily varnished, like covers or the Playboy centerfold. The fresher the ink, the better.

2. Select paper or cloth

Paper: This should be as smooth as possible because textured papers cause the image to look blurry.

Cloth: The best results I've seen have been on a thick acetate satin. A smooth tightly woven fabric is best.

3. Select an ink solvent.

A variety of solvents will work including silkscreen transparent base, lighter fluid, Carbona spot remover, and offset lithography blanket wash. Transparent base is the easiest to control, the most economical, and produces fewest fumes. It's available at art supply stores and any brand will work. If you can afford it, buy halftone screen base as it works the best.

METAL SPOON METHOD

Tape your paper on a hard surface face up. Tape magazine image to it face down. You may wish to mask around the magazine image with newsprint. Apply a teaspoon full of transparent base to the back of the magazine image and spread it around until the solvent begins to penetrate the paper. Rub hard with a metal spoon, checking your results by lifting one corner of the magazine image up periodically. Be patient, this may take 15 minutes.

Most images will transfer by this method. Remember that a varnished image will not rub off (because this solvent won't dissolve varnish). The slight color shift occurs because you have reversed the color layers that the printer printed. You have also reversed the image.

ETCHING PRESS METHOD I

Place paper or cloth face up on the press bed. Tape magazine image face down and begin to spread the transparent base on the back of it. As the ink begins to dissolve, wipe the excess off and place a blotter on top to protect the felts. Run the entire stack through the press. You should get a crisp, perfectly even transfer of ink onto your chosen material. If not, increase the pressure or allow the solvent more time to work.

ETCHING PRESS METHOD II

Lay the *magazine image* face up on the press bed. Mist the front of the magazine image with Carbona spot remover. The mist must be very fine, so use a small pressurized sprayer with an attached glass jar (available in most hardware stores). Very quickly place your paper or fabric on top of the magazine image. Add a blotter to this to protect the felts. Run it through the press.

This method yields beautiful results on fabric. You must work very fast as the spot remover dissolves the ink immediately. You may need a friend to help you. Also be sure to work with adequate ventilation.

MAGAZINE LIFTS WITH CONTACT PAPER

This method will lift the ink off clay coated magazine paper.

It is cheap, but requires more labor than the "Flexible Acrylic Lifts" described next in this book.

1. Select a magazine image and lay it face up on a counter. Only unvarnished ink images printed on clay coated paper will work. Images printed on newsprint will not work.
2. Adhere clear Contact Paper to the front of this image.
This plastic coat must now be rubbed very hard with a metal spoon or burnisher, or if possible, run it through an etching press. This pressure forces the ink into the adhesive layer of the Contact paper.
3. Soak magazine page and Contact paper in hot water
The magazine paper and the clay coating dissolve in water leaving the ink stuck to the Contact paper.
4. Hang to Dry
5. Suggestions for use
Contact print this clear lift onto ortho film to make a negative.
Mount pieces of lift into slide mounts. These slides could then be used in slide shows, or projected in special attachments to make large color Xerox images.

FLEXIBLE MAGAZINE LIFTS WITH ACRYLIC MEDIUM

It is possible to "lift" the ink off a printed clay coated magazine page with acrylic medium. The result is a flexible transparent image. It can be distorted if desired. It can be contact printed onto ortho film to make a negative, or it can be used in the same way a positive ortho film image is used.

1. Select clay coated magazine image
Note that this process will not work on varnished images or on newsprint images. Start with Newsweek or Time as their inner pages are printed on a coated stock called clay coated paper.

2. Coat the front side of the image with gloss acrylic medium
Apply the gloss acrylic medium (Hyplar, Liquitex, Aquatex) with a wide paint brush. After this coat is dry, repeat this process at least 8 times. Paint the medium on in different directions each time. You can force dry the layers, but it is better to coat a large group at a time over a period of hours and do something else between coats.

3. Soak entire coated page in hot (or hot soapy) water
The hot water penetrates the paper and eventually dissolves the clay coated layer, leaving only the printer's ink in the acrylic film that you have constructed. To completely dissolve the clay layer, you may need to rub the back of the image gently. Some printing papers separate more easily than others.
Note: The acrylic coat turns milky white when wet, but it will clear again when it dries.

4. Hang to dry

5. Suggestions for use:
You may wish to distort this image. This is accomplished most easily by cutting the image into a shape of some sort, prewarming it with a hair drier, and laying it face down on some acetate or glass. Begin to stretch it from its edges, but don't force it too far, or it will snap. You should be able to distort it by about 30%. This stretched image on the acetate may be used to make a cyanotype, Kwik Print, etc., but because it is a positive image you will get a negative result.
   This lift may be contact printed onto ortho film in a darkroom. This will give you the required negative and in most cases it will be a halftone negative because the original magazine image was printed in halftone dots.
   The lift can also be warmed and stretched around three dimensional objects like clay pots. It is so flexible that it will conform to almost any surface!
   The lift can be stuffed and stitched into original art pieces.

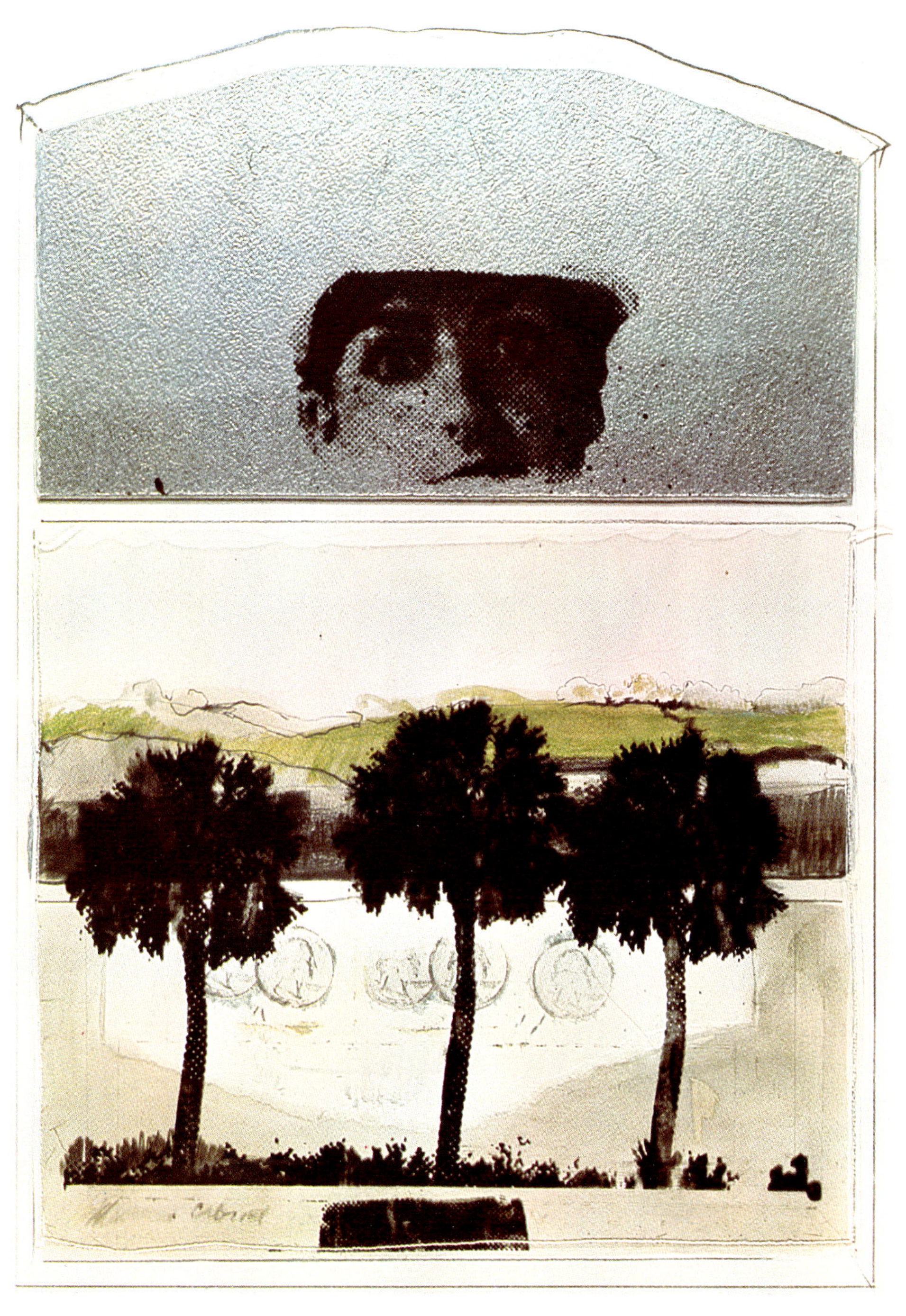

"Seeing all these things, she stored them in her medicine cabinet," Drawing, magazine rubbings and silkscreen on paper and vinyl, 12" x 16", 1970.

CYANOTYPE

The cyanotype (blue image on a white ground) is an old photographic process which is quite useful today. It uses 2 chemicals available from scientific chemical companies. It works well on paper and natural fibers like cotton, silk and canvas.

STOCK SOLUTIONS: *May be stored in dark bottles for months.*

A. **Ferric Ammonium Citrate**   50 grams to 8 oz. distilled water
(green crystals)

B. **Potassium Ferricyanide**   35 grams to 8 oz. distilled water

1. Mix equal volumes A and B. Use this the same day.

2. Sensitize surface
Soak paper or fabric in a tray of solution or apply it with a brush. This should be done under dim roomlight.

3. Dry coated material
This should be done under dim light with a hair drier or fan. If you leave material to air dry, it is best to leave it in total darkness. Coating should dry a bright yellow.

4. Expose
Contact print your sensitized material through a negative. Even continuous tone negatives will work if you have a very strong light source.

Blue prints need a lot of light. Strong sunlight is best, next would be carbon arc or flourescent black light tubes, and last resorts are sunlamps and quartz lamps.

Test your light to determine exposure time; longer exposures yield darker blues. During exposure the coated material should change from a light green to a bluish grey and finally to a blue green. It is rare that you will overexpose a high contrast or halftone negative. Timing should be more careful with continuous tone negatives.

5. Wash
Wash in running water until yellow stain is gone. If the blue washes off, you've underexposed the print. If a blue stain remains in the highlights, the print may have been overexposed or fogged during application.

6. (Optional) Intensification
To slightly darken the blue and brighten the highlights, the print may be dipped in a weak solution of Clorox and water (1/32). Immerse it for a few seconds only, then rinse print 15-30 minutes more.

7. Dry
Image will appear darker when it is dry.

8. Second coat?
This unfortunately doesn't work well, as the new coat bleaches out the first image.

VAN DYKE BROWN PRINTING

Ferric Ammonium Citrate	90 grams
Tartaric Acid	15 grams
Silver Nitrate	37.5 grams or 1 oz. bottle
Distilled Water	

1. Mix stock solution
Mix each of the chemicals separately in 8 ounces of distilled water. Combine the Ferric Ammonium Citrate and the Tartaric Acid solutions and slowly add the Silver Nitrate solution. Add distilled water to make 32 ounces of solution. Store this in a brown bottle in a dark place. It should be good for many months.
   CAUTION: Wear gloves during the mixing because Silver Nitrate causes burns and can penetrate through the skin.

2. Sensitize surface
Artists' paper or organic fabric (cotton, linen, silk) can be dipped in a solution or it can be brushed on these materials.
   Coat as evenly as possible. **Don't get it on your hands!** Brown print solution on the hands results in unattractive and unhealthy stains.

3. Dry
Hang to dry or use a hair drier.

4. Expose
Contact print your sensitized material through any type of negative. This solution is about 3 times as light sensitive as Cyanotype. Sunlight will work in as little as 1 minute and other light sources will work with corresponding speed.

5. Wash
After exposure, wash the sensitized material for about 5 minutes in running water. Absorbent cloth or paper should be washed even longer or stains will appear later. An orange-brown print is the result.

6. Fix
The print can now be immersed briefly in a tray of water containing a small amount of regular paper fixer (1 part fixer to 20 parts water). This will change the image color to a dark brown. This also tends to brighten the highlights. Don't leave the print in the fixer long after it has turned dark brown as it will begin to bleach out.

7. Final Wash
Print may be hypo-cleared to shorten the final washing time to 15 minutes. Otherwise, wash the print about 30 minutes.

8. Dry
The print will darken slightly as it dries.

9. Second coat?
This usually won't work very well, and results in stains.

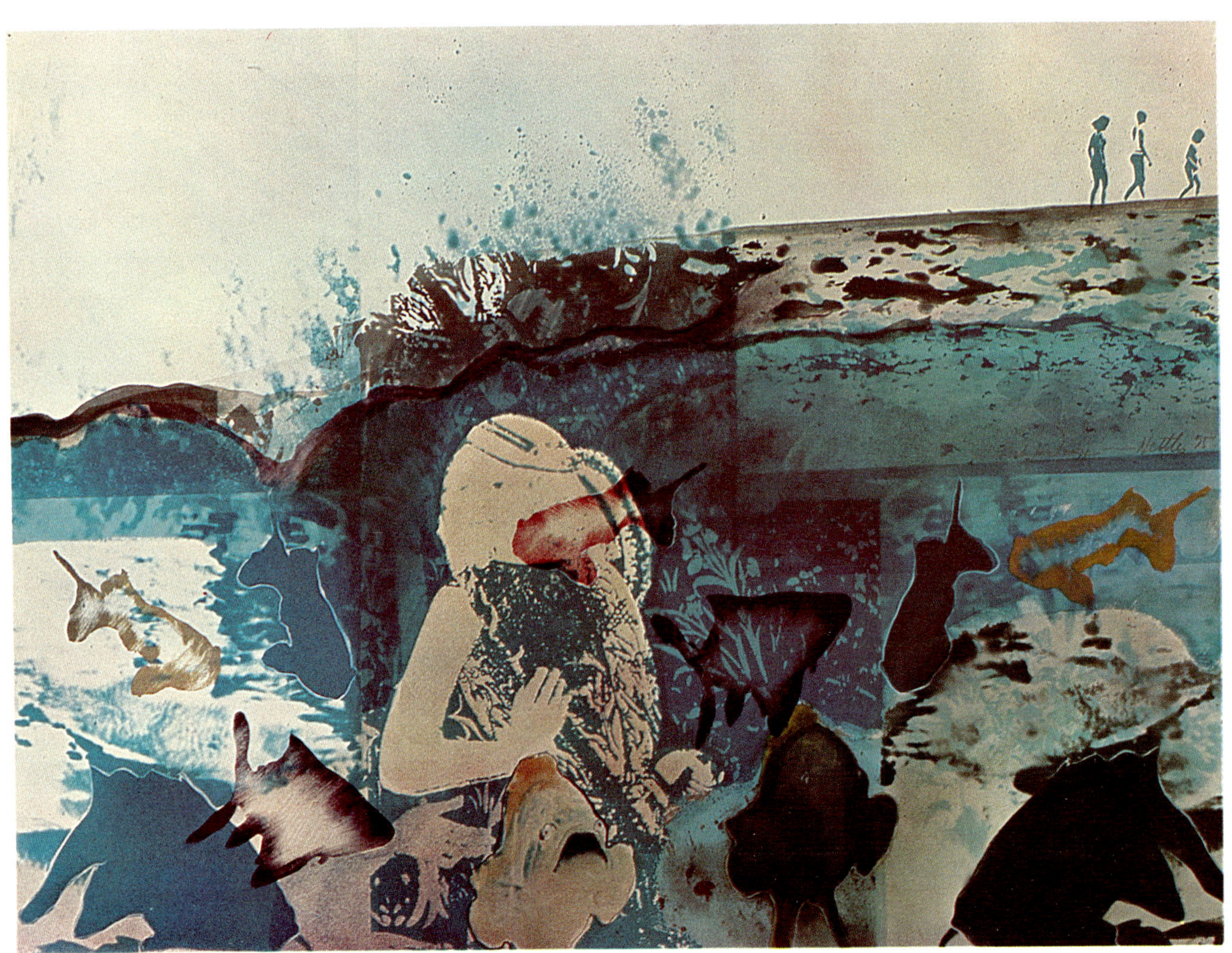

"Fish Fantasy," cyanotype and color pencil on paper, 19" x 26", 1975.

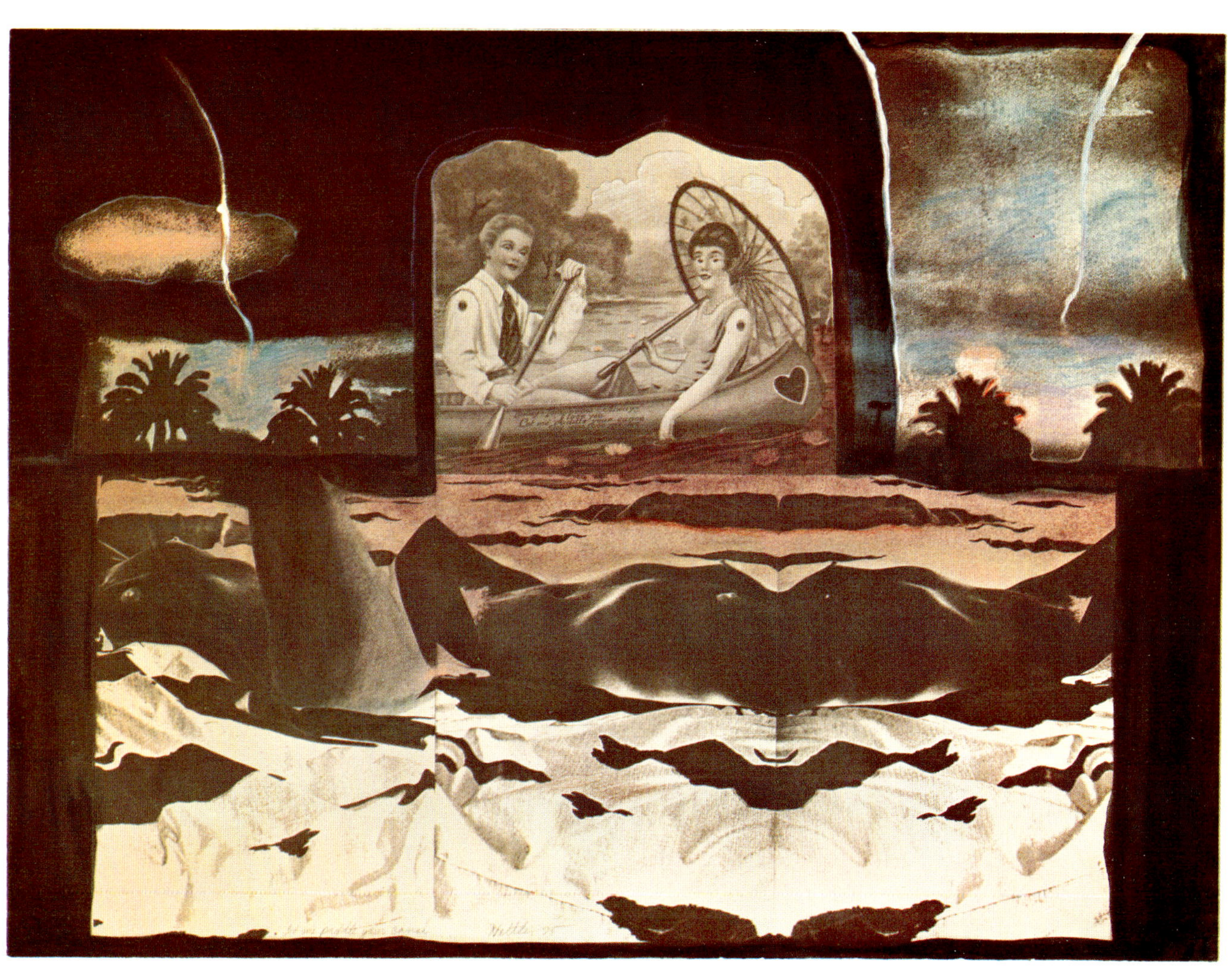

"Let Me Paddle Your Canoe."   *Van Dyke brown print and oil paint on paper, 19'' x 26'', 1975.*

KWIK PRINT

This is a graphic arts product used for proofing offset negatives before a color printing job goes to press. Until 1977 it was marketed as "Kwik Proof." It is extremely versatile, economical, permanent, and readily available to the photographic artist. The entire process can be done under dim room light with simple equipment.

It is designed for use on vinyl sheets, but can be used on artist's paper and fabric, as will be described later.

Source: **Light Impressions Corporation**
131 Gould Street
Rochester, N.Y. 14610
(Write for a catalog and complete instructions. There is a trial kit available with everything you need to get started but an exposure light)

Materials needed:

Kwik Print Sheets — Dimensionally stable vinyl sheets. Available in many sizes up to 54" x 75". Comes in 2 thicknesses: .005 and .01 ml.

Kwik Print Colors — Light sensitive colored liquids, In 40 colors and clear.

Cotton pads or Webril Wipes

Kwik Print Brightener or Household ammonia

Contact size negatives — High contrast, random or halftone dot and continuous tone.

Light source — Sun, carbon arc, quartz, sunlamp, photoflood.

HOW TO USE KWIK PRINT ON KWIK PRINT SHEETS

1. Prepare Kwik Print Sheet

The sheet is white vinyl. It is not light sensitive, but it has a coating on one side that makes the colors stick. Sprinkle some water on a hard smooth counter surface and lay the sheet face up, pressing it down with your hands so that the sheet sticks to the counter.

This eliminates the need to tape the sheet down and lets you work all the way out to the edges. Wipe off any excess water on coating area with a paper towel.

2. Select first Kwik Print color

If you buy red, blue, yellow, black, and clear, you can intermix any color you like. (You can also buy only clear and add your own watercolor pigment; this is not as convenient and less predictable).

It is easiest to register later colors if you start with a dark color on the first coating. Shake the bottle and pour a small amount on the sheet. If you wish to mix a color, pour small quantities into a plastic cup and mix. These colors will last several hours under roomlight. Eventually they will dry out and should be washed out of the cups.

3. Coat the sheet

Usually on the first exposure you will want to coat the entire sheet. Tear a cotton pad into strips and fold it up. With it wipe the Kwik Print color over the entire sheet. Use a clean cotton pad to buff the coat dry. I use the Kwik Print Applipad if I am coating a very large area. This is perhaps the most critical step. You want an even, thin coat with no streaks. (If you do get streaks, wash the sheet off with water, dry it, and start over...because streaks will show).

As there is a drier in Kwik Print, you will have to work fast. The speed with which it dries will be one of the great advantages of this product, after you have acquired the coating skill. It's a good idea to expose the sheet shortly after coating because Kwik Print acquires its light sensitivity as it dries, but even then normal room light for short periods of time will not fog the emulsion.

4. Choose negative

Lay a contact size negative on the coated sheet. Any good negative will work. With one continuous tone negative you can get a wide range of tones by deliberately over and under exposing the various color layers.

You can also use photogram materials such as spray paint on acetate, drawing on acetate, lace, leaves, etc.

5. Expose

It is best to use a vacuum frame. Next best is a contact frame, but even a sheet of glass and a foam coated backing board will work. Kwik Print doesn't need very long exposures. You will need to experiment to determine what is best with your light source. You can use sun, carbon arc, quartz lights, sunlamps, or photofloods (listed in the order of intensity).

On the first exposure, I often deliberately underexpose the negative. In this way I can add additional detail in lighter colors later.

6. Develop

Take the Kwik Print sheet to a sink and hose it with tap water. The unexposed color and its bichromate sensitizer will wash off. If you have difficulty getting the color to wash off after about 2 minutes, spray the surface with some weak ammoniated water. I mix a few tablespoons of household ammonia in a quart of water and keep it in a plastic spray bottle for this purpose. Kwik Print Brightener can also be used, but it is very strong and can remove many color layers if not used with care.

At this point you can deliberately remove areas of color with a sponge and scouring powder or a typing eraser. When well exposed the color layer is surprisingly tough. It can be accidentally scratched, however, with a fingernail or ring, and if this happens you will be unable to coat any color in that area because you have removed the chemical coating from the sheet and have exposed the bare vinyl. When the print is finished you can try to retouch the scratch with color pencils.

7. Dry
Hang the sheet to dry or dry it with a soft cloth if you're in a rush.

8. Additional Color layers
You can add as many color layers as you wish. The sheet will not shrink or curl up, enabling you to get perfect registration. Often I add color only in specific areas, carefully wiping off excess with a damp piece of cotton or masking out areas with goldenrod masking paper before exposure.

   Real richness is built up by using many layers of color. Colors are translucent, so remember this when mixing color. This product was designed to proof four color separation negatives and a full color print can be obtained in this way.

9. Addition of other media
The finished print can be painted on or drawn on with color pencils. You can even draw on it during the process with wax crayons or pencils. This gives an interesting effect, because the wax resists the Kwik Print applied over it.

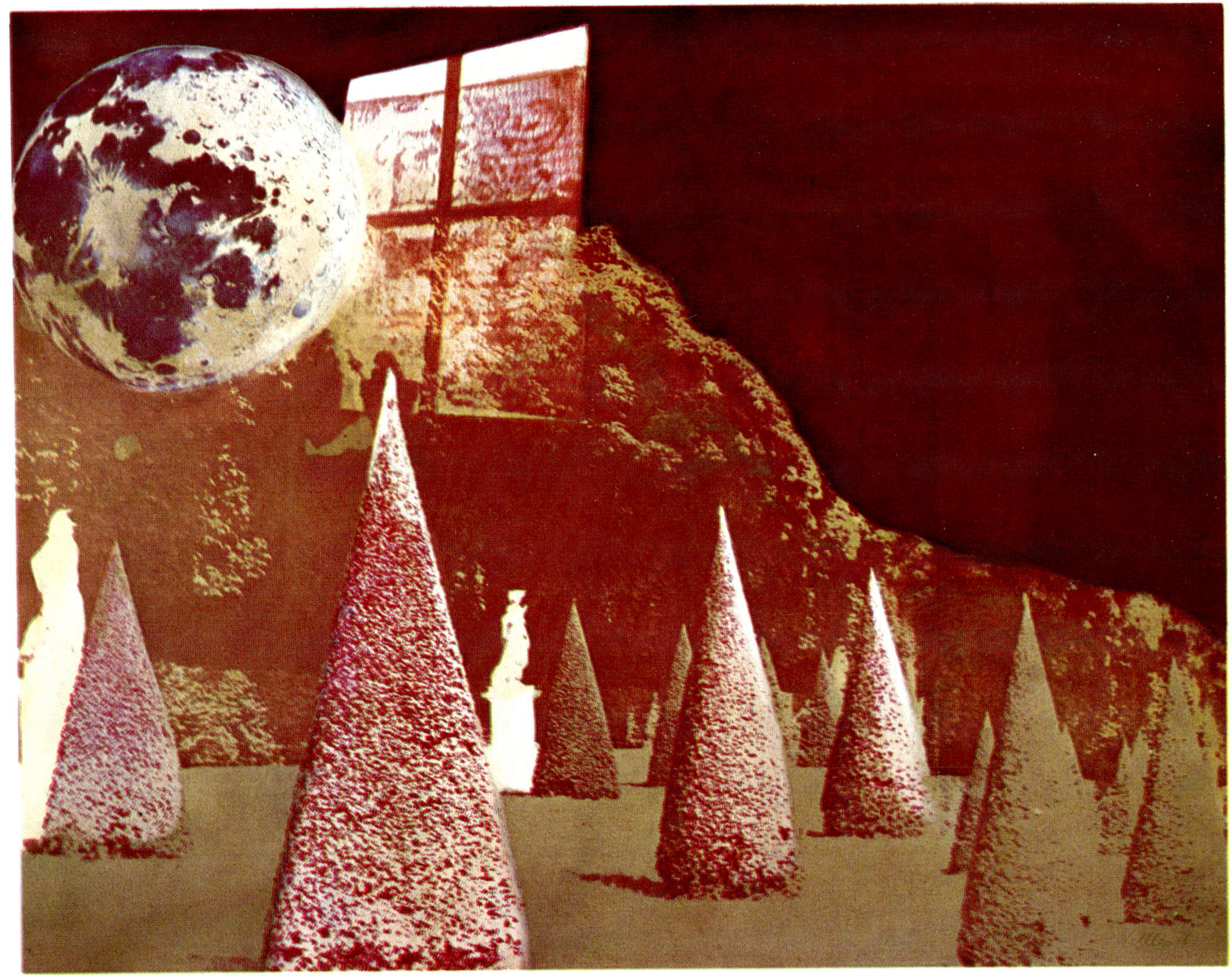

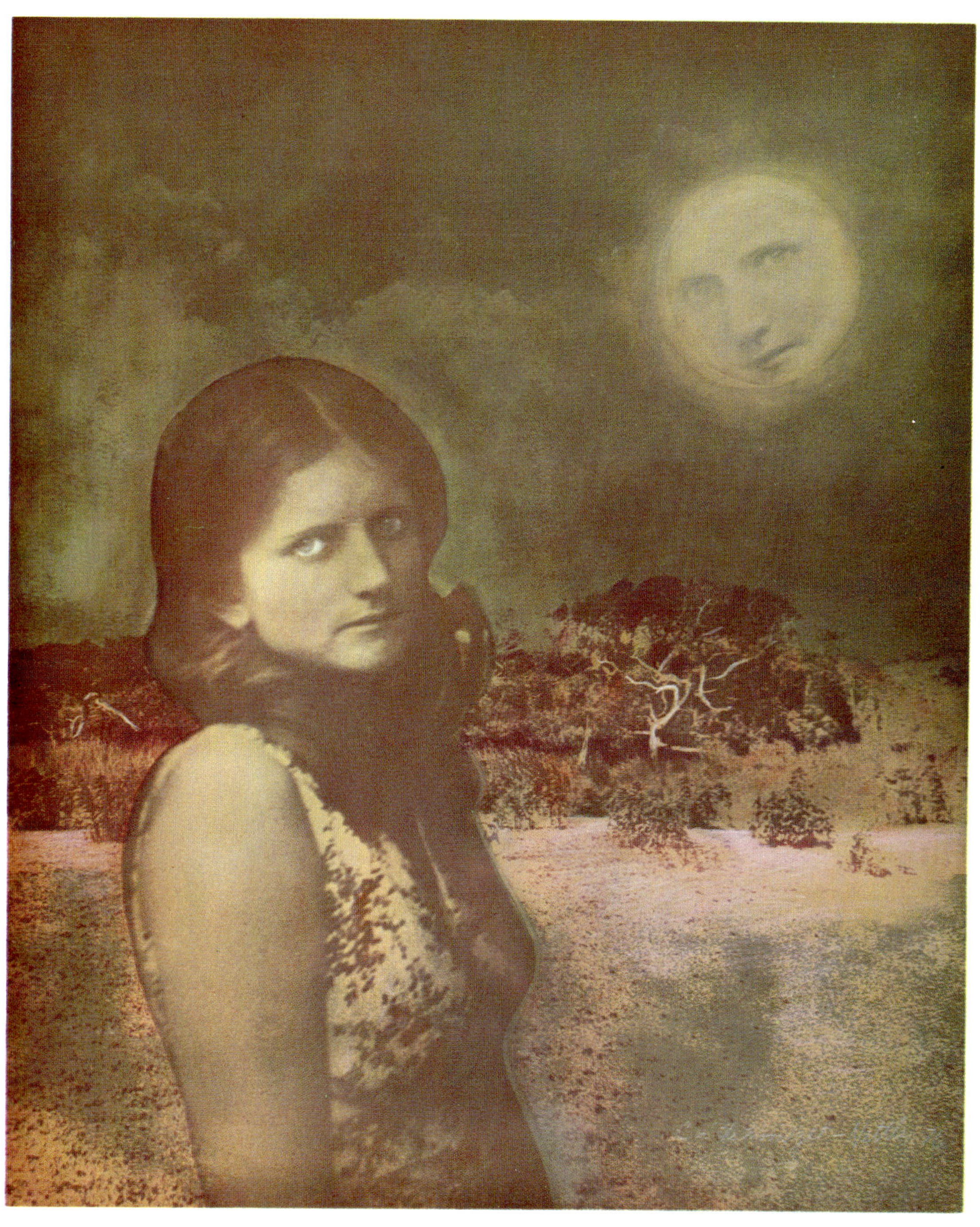

"Connie in the Moonlight," Kwik Print on vinyl, 15" x 18", 1976.

OPPOSITE PAGE: "Versailles," Kwik Print on vinyl, 20" x 26", 1976.

KWIK PRINT ON ARTIST'S PAPER

Kwik Print was designed to coat plastic sheets, but if paper is treated it can be used with Kwik Print colors to achieve some very beautiful results. I feel that it is much simpler and more versatile than gum printing. For this reason I am not describing the gum printing process in this book.

1. Prepare the Paper
Choose a good quality artist's paper that can be soaked in water (Rives, Arches, or Gallery from Light Impressions).
   Pre-shrink it by soaking it in a tray of hot water, removing it and letting it air dry.
   Size it with dilute Elmer's Glue or acrylic medium. Brush the sizing on evenly and let the sheet dry.

2. Coat the paper
Mix any color Kwik Print that you wish. Brush it on the sized paper surface as evenly as possible with a wide paint brush. Kwik Print color can also be airbrushed onto the paper if you have that equipment.

3. Dry the paper
Hang the paper to dry in a dark space, or blow dry it in subdued light. Be sure it is truly dry, or your exposure will be uneven.

4. Expose
You may use any negative material, but your exposures may be slightly longer than they were on a Kwik Print vinyl sheet because the paper is more absorbent.

5. Develop
Wash the sheet in running water. Rub surface gently with a sponge or brush, but don't be afraid to apply moderate pressure if needed. It may be necessary to clear the highlights with ammoniated water.

6. Dry paper
Hang it to air dry or force it dry with a hair drier or fan.

7. Additional colors
Follow the above steps with additional colors. Any color can be mixed. It is possible to get very saturated color by coating and exposing the same area with the same color twice.

KWIK PRINT ON FABRIC

Kwik Print works beautifully on fabric and yields a permanent, washable result in any color you wish.

1. Select the fabric
Choose a synthetic fiber with a smooth surface. Satin (100% acetate) and crepe work beautifully. Iron it well.

(If you wish to work with an organic fiber like cotton or even a cotton/polyester blend, it is best to starch the fabric before coating it, dry it and iron it.)

2. Mix Kwik Print Color
Best results can be obtained by mixing one part Kwik Print color with 2 parts Kwik Print clear. Otherwise, the fabric gets over-saturated and it is difficult to clear the highlights.

A bit of water can be added to this mixture if a slight stiffness in the image area would be a problem. The water should be used only if you feel that the fabric is made too stiff by the Kwik Print, because the addition of water makes it more difficult to get clear highlights.

3. Coat fabric
Lay fabric on a smooth clean surface. Brush the color onto the fabric with a wide paintbrush.

4. Dry fabric
If the coating has not saturated through the back of the fabric, it can be left to air dry on a flat surface in the dark. It is also possible to hang the fabric in a dark place to dry . Usually some color will concentrate along the bottom edge, but this can be eliminated if the fabric is given an initial "blow drying" with a hair drier. This will set the Kwik Print up enough so that it won't flow down through fabric that is hung to dry.

5. Expose
For fabric, it is quite important to have a vacuum frame to assure perfectly sharp imagery. Next best is a contact frame. Exposures may be longer than on a Kwik Print vinyl sheet because of the saturation of the fabric.

6. Wash the fabric
Place the fabric in a tray or bucket of water. Wash the initial unexposed areas out and pour washwater down the drain. Fabric may be scrubbed, folded, rubbed with a brush or hands with no damage to the image if it was given sufficient exposure.

If you have difficulty clearing highlights, dip the fabric into a bath of dilute ammoniated water, then rub some more. Wash out may take several minutes.

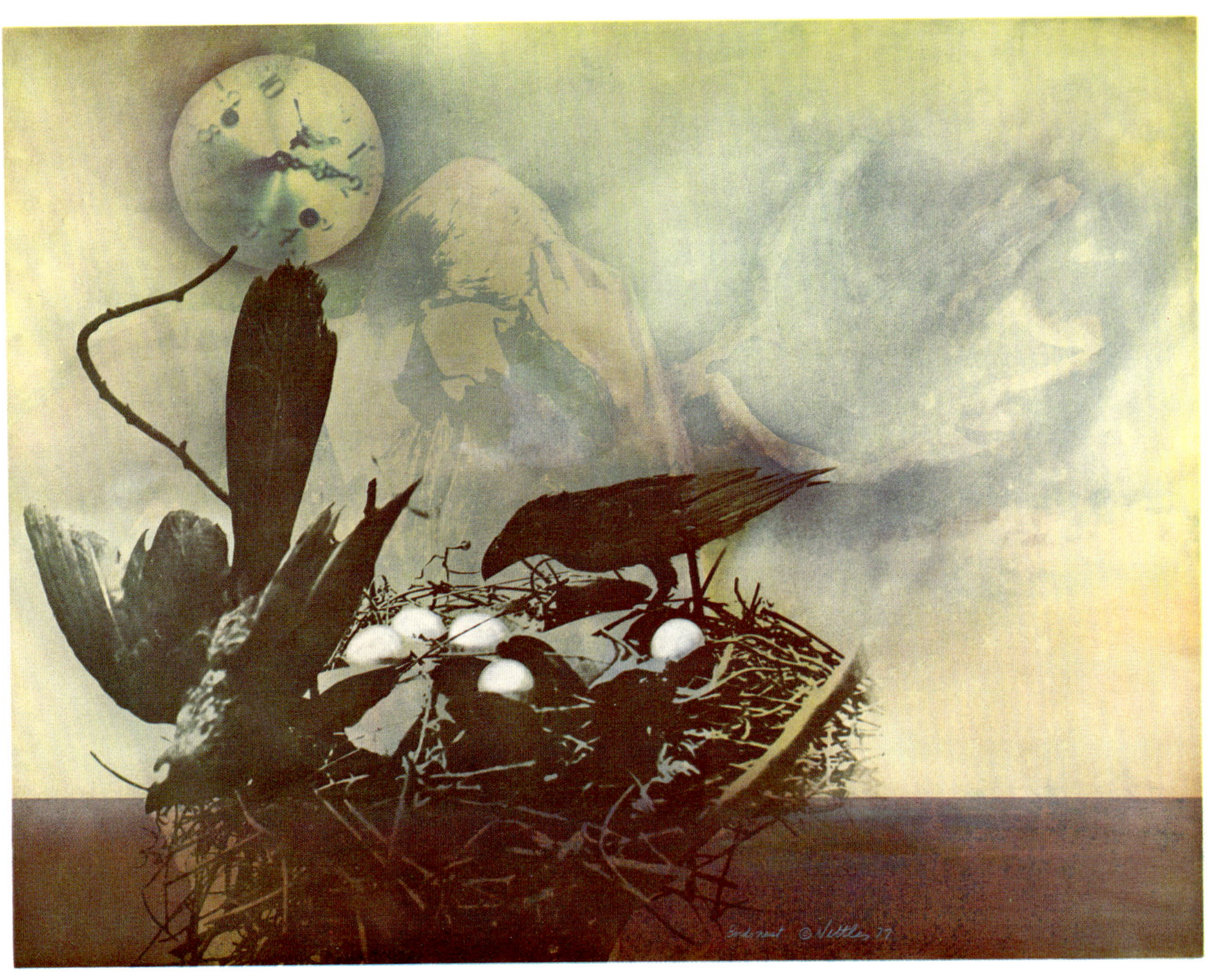

7. Dry fabric
Hang on the line to dry, or iron it dry if you're in a hurry.

8. Additional Colors
After the first color is dry, a second color may be applied. As with Kwik Print on paper or vinyl, you may coat the entire area or selectively paint it on. Dry the new color, expose, wash out, etc.

The main difficulty with fabric is achieving perfect registration. If perfection is your goal, it would be wise to preshrink the fabric. Then, either stretch it using a staple gun onto a waterproof board, or sew the fabric into a "pillowcase" and slip it very tightly over a waterproof board or a bit of plexiglass. Leave the fabric thus stretched out during all coating, drying, exposing and washing until the image is finished.

9. Permanence
Kwik Prints on fabric can be machine washed often and are light fast.

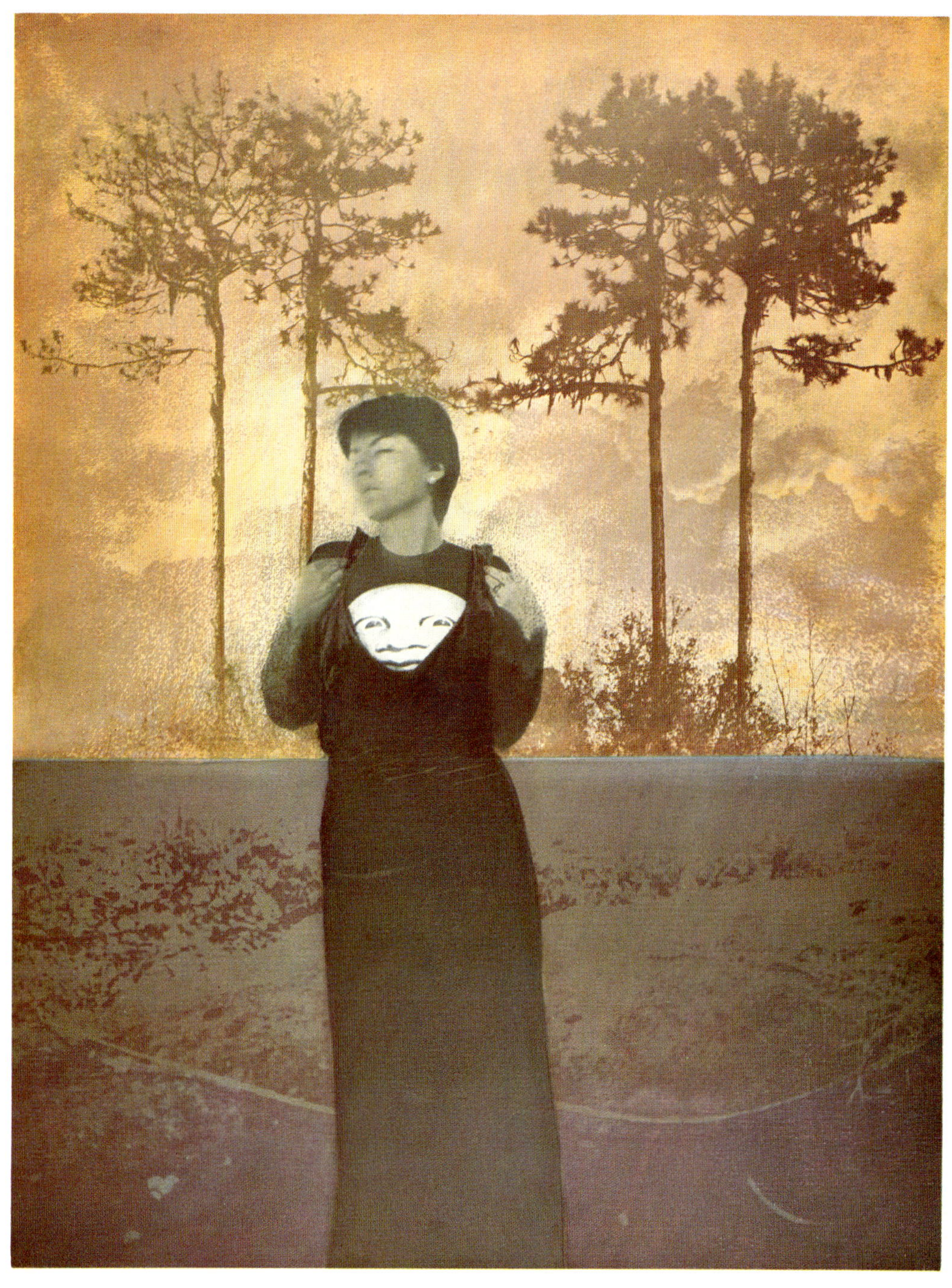

"Moonrise thru the Pines," Kwik Print on vinyl, 20" x 26", 1976.

OPPOSITE PAGE: "Birdsnest," Kwik Print on vinyl, 20" x 26", 1977.

HAND COLORING PHOTOGRAPHIC SURFACES

Many materials can be used to hand color photographic surfaces. They are divided into three categories, depending on their solvents: oil based, lacquer based, and water based. These materials can be used in combination on photographic surfaces. But as in all painting, remember that oil and lacquer based materials will adhere to water based ones, while water based materials don't work well over oil and lacquer based ones.

1. *Oil based materials*
These were some of the first materials used for hand coloring photographic prints. They remain the easiest to control and are a good way to start out. Any artist's oil paint will work well on almost any photographic surface. It helps to prime the surface with a fine film of turpentine rubbed on with cotton. A surface thus prepared is easy to color with traditional color pencils, Marshall oil color pencils, or oil paint.

A soft, subtle color is characteristic of oil toning. Large areas such as skies are easily blended with cotton or fingers. Because it takes a long time to dry, mistakes can be "erased" with turpentine and cotton.

When dry, oil color is the most permanent of the hand toning methods.

2. *Lacquer based spray paint*
Spray paint can be very useful on photographic surfaces. The surface can be sprayed in an overall area or partially masked. If you don't wish to use spray cans, an air brush can produce some very beautiful results on photographs.

3. *Water based materials*
Although there are many types of water based coloring materials, they fall into the basic categories listed below. Some methods require skill which should be acquired by practicing on test prints.

ADDITIVE (LOCAL) COLOR:
Marshall Photo Retouch Colors
Concentrated Edwal Toners
Acrylic Paints

These materials are generally used on dry photographic surfaces. Various sizes of camel's hair brushes are used for application, The **Marshall** or **Edwal** colors can be used straight out of the bottle, or can be mixed and intermixed to form different colors on a glass palette. If the colors on the palette dry out, they can be "reconstituted" by touching them with a wet paint brush. For this reason, there is very little waste and they are quite economical.

Color added in this direct way can be intense or subtle depending on the amount of water used. The application of these direct colors requires confidence and skill, because once the brush has touched the photograph, the color penetrates the surface and is permanent (as happens when you "spot" a black and white photograph). If you're trying to paint large areas, it helps to dip your brush in some diluted photo-flo first.

To paint large areas you must work very fast if you don't want the brush strokes to show. It may help if you wet the entire photographic surface if you wish to color large areas.

A print colored in this method is often brighter and clearer than an oil toned print. This is because the colors are concentrated and they soak into the surface of the print, unlike oil color which tends to sit on the surface.

Acrylic paint can also be used for additive color. It has the advantage of a comparatively slow drying time which means it can be removed while still wet with some cotton soaked in water. Acrylics always sit on the surface of the print and have the definite appearance of paint added over an image. If this is not objectionable, then you will find acrylics very permanent and easy to work with.

OVERALL TONERS:
Kodak Brown, Blue, Sepia Toners
Edwal Photo Toners
Dye

To use these materials, it is necessary to immerse the entire print (or photo aluminum, photo linen, etc.) into a bath of toner. Mix these toners according to the manufacturer's directions. When used properly, the **Kodak** color toners wash completely out of the highlights of the print and are quite permanent. The **Edwal** blue and green toners wash out best, while the red, yellow and brown toners tend to leave a slight tint in the highlights. (Edwal toned prints of mine have changed color over the years, but I was using them in higher concentrations than were recommended).

Commercial fabric **dyes** can be used on photographs, but they will stain the highlights because they give an overall tone to the entire print.

It is possible to mask out certain areas of a photographic surface with rubber cement or "Maskoid". After masking in this manner, the print is immersed in a tray of toner, toned, rinsed off, and then the masking solution is rubbed off the surface leaving that area black and white. After a print is given an overall tone, it is possible to do some additional hand coloring on the surface with water based colors while the surface is still wet. After the surface is dry, oil based materials may be used as a final step.

BLEACH:
Potassium Ferricyanide

A dilute Potassium Ferricyanide solution (about 1 teaspoon to 16 ounces of water is fine) can be used for a variety of effects. Use Q Tips or a soft brush containing no metal for application. Bleach is usually applied to a wet print. As the image approaches the desired result, the print is immersed in a tray of fixer to stop the bleaching action.

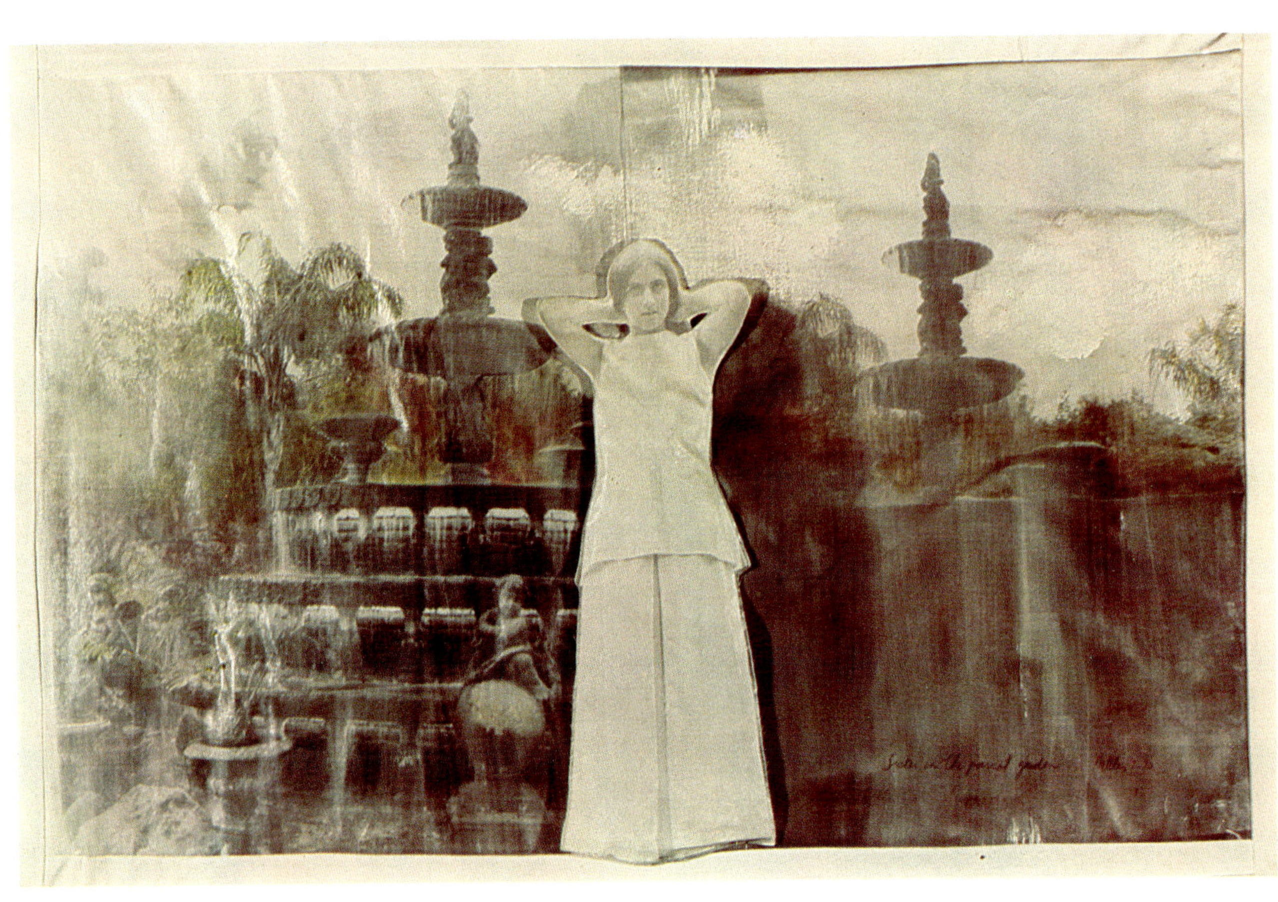

"Sister in the Parrot Garden," Hand toned Rockland Emulsion on cloth with machine stitching. 19" x 30", 1970.

The print is then rewashed before anything else is done to it. Very painterly results can be obtained by deliberate bleaching of image areas. Bleach can also be controlled so that the effect is very subtle.

When using some of the Kodak toners, the entire print is bleached and then immersed in toner. Why not bleach the print and then paint back into it with toner in selected areas? Or try bleaching only parts of the print, using a mask or selectively brushing the bleach on, then toning only those bleached sections?

Hand coloring photo surfaces can be very exciting. Many combinations are possible. The chart on coloring gives you some idea of the materials you might choose for different surfaces.

The symbols in the chart are: (+) positive results, (L) limited results, and (-) poor or negative results.

	Pencil	Oil paint	Spray paint	Acrylic paint	Marshall colors	Edwal toners	Dye	Bleach
Matte photo	+	+	+	+	+	+	+	+
Gloss photo	L	+	+	+	+	+	+	+
RC photo	-	-	+	+	+	L	-	+
Photo Linen	+	+	+	+	+	+	+	+
Photo Aluminum	L	L	+	L	+	+	-	+
Rockland Emulsion	+	+	+	+	+	+	+	+
Kwik Print	+	+	+	+	-	-	-	-
Cyanotype	+	+	+	+	-	-	+	+
Brown Print	+	+	+	+	-	-	+	+
Screen Print	+	+	+	+	-	-	L	-
Ortho Film	-	+	+	L	+	+	L	+
Magazine Rubbing	+	+	+	L	-	-	L	-
Magazine Lift	-	-	+	+	-	-	-	-
Etched Glass	-	+	+	L	-	-	-	-

PHOTO SCREEN PRINTING

There are many good manuals dealing with this process and most products come with fine instructions. A basic outline of the two main methods of photo screen printing is below, mainly to give you an idea of what is involved. Check the comparison table to determine which method is right for your purpose.

METHOD 1: PHOTO FILM TYPE SCREENS

Supplies needed:
Ulano Presensitized Screen Fotofilm (either Blue Poly or HiFi Green)
Ulano A B HiFi Prep Developer
Ulano Microgrit (fine abrasive powder)
Ortho film positive
Contact Frame and exposure light
Newsprint
Stretched screen

Prepare Screen:
Buy polyester monofilament that is fine enough for the image you plan to use. 200-240 mesh is commonly used. Stretch it with a staple gun to a wooden frame. Pre-roughen and degrease new screen with Ulano Microgrit. Scouring powder will work in a pinch, but it will clog a very fine screen.

Choose Positive Image:
High Contrast ortho
Random or Halftone Dot ortho (remember if you use a very fine dot you will need an even finer mesh screen.)
Magazine Lift
Drawing on Acetate

Putting the image on the Screen:
 1. Cut the Ulano film slightly larger than your image.
    You may handle this film under dim roomlight.

 2. Place Ulano film and positive image in contact frame.
    The Ulano film *must be exposed through its acetate backing.*

Top	Glass
↓	Positive film image, emulsion side up (as you look at image from the light source, it should be backwards)
Bottom	Ulano film (shiny acetate side touches ortho, dull emulsion side is away from light source.

3. Expose
   Do a test strip to determine time with your exposure light:

   Sun   8 minutes
   Carbon Arc   4 minutes
   Photo Flood   20 minutes

4. Mix Developer
   Ulano HiFi Prep Developer parts A and B are added to 16 ounces of water
   not above 75 degrees. You may make your own developer from 35%
   Hydrogen Peroxide mixed 1 ounce to 20 ounces of water. Pour the
   developer into a tray and keep it covered from strong light and discard it at
   the end of the day.

5. Develop Ulano film
   Insert film in developer tray emulsion side up. Agitate it for 1½ minutes. You
   won't see an image.

6. Wash in Hot Water
   Lay Ulano film on a flat surface emulsion side up. Spray it with hot water
   until excess gelatin comes off. Image will appear in the negative.

7. Immerse Ulano in Cold Water to set gelatin.

8. Transfer to screen.
   Lay Ulano film emulsion side UP on newsprint on a smooth surface. Lay the
   screen on top of this film in correct position. Blot the screen with newsprint
   from the center out until no more color or moisture is absorbed by the
   newsprint. The gelatin is in this way forced into the fibers of the screen.
   (Optional) Block out edges with water soluble glue.

9. Air dry the screen about 1 hour until the acetate backing looks frosted.

10. Peel acetate backing off the screen gently. Clean the screen with lacquer
    thinner to remove any excess gelatin.

11. Screen is now ready to print with oil based inks only.

12. When you wish to clean the photo image off the screen entirely, it may be
    scrubbed out with a brush and hot soapy water.

Entire process may be repeated again and again with new images.

Method 2: Direct Emulsions

Supplies needed:

Stretched screen (monofillament 200-240 mesh polyester)
Squeegee
Light source and piece of glass
Ortho Film positive
Direct Emulsion
    Commercial Direct Emulsion: NazDar no. 32 EZ Direct Photo Emulsion

Homemade Direct Emulsion:

To make your own, add one level tablespoon Knox gelatin to 2 ounces cold water. Let this stand 10 minutes then place this mixture in a container set inside a beaker of hot water. After the gelatin has completely dissolved, add a small amount of watercolor to it to aid its visibility. Then add 1 gram of Ammonium Dichromate to each ounce of liquid gelatin you have prepared. This mixture is now light sensitive and should be used immediately.

Basic Procedure:

1. Prepare stretched screen and roughen and degrease it. Dry the screen well.
2. Under dim lights or yellow bug light, coat the emulsion onto the back of the screen. Special squeegees called "coaters" (see NazDar catalog) are great for this purpose, but you can use a regular squeegee. Coat two thin layers in opposite directions, allowing the layers to dry between coats.
3. Expose Emulsion Coated Screen. After placing the positive ortho image on the emulsion side of the screen, lay glass over it to hold it in contact. You may need to pad the screen from underneath to build up contact. Expose with a bright light source (sun, carbon arc, sunlamp, quartz light, photofloods).
4. Develop the image by spraying hot water through the screen washing away unexposed emulsion.
5. Air dry the screen.
6. Print with any type of ink (oil or water based).
7. To remove image from the screen use the proper solvent. Chlorine bleach will remove Homemade Emulsion. Hydrogen Peroxide will remove NazDar Emulsion.

PHOTO SCREEN METHODS: COMPARISON

	Ulano Films	*Direct Emulsions*
Cost	Expensive	Cheap
Ink	Oil based only	Oil or water based materials (useful for ceramic glazes, glass etch, Inkodye, and all screen inks)
Exposure	Easily determined with a test strip	difficult to determine (if you make a mistake you must wash the emulsion out of the screen)
Time	Entire process can be finished in less than 1 hour	Process takes several hours because 2 coats of emulsion must dry before exposure, and again after development.
Detail	Can render the finest detail if exposed properly	Can render the finest detail if exposed properly.
Clean out	Easily cleaned out of screens with water.	Requires a chemical for clean out.
Screen fiber	Works well on silk or polyester	Use with polyester only, as clean out chemicals will destroy silk.

PROCESS COMPARISON CHART

	Comparative Exposures	Color Range	Surfaces	Health Hazards
Kwik Print	2 minutes full sun	all	Vinyl sheets. Sized paper. Synthetic fabric.	Bichromate in KP liquids and wash water.
Gum Printing	5 minutes full sun	all (some are very difficult to obtain)	Paper. Sized organic fabric	Bichromate in coating mix and wash water.
Cyanotype	6-10 minutes full sun	blue/white	Paper. Organic fabric.	Chemicals in coating and wash water.
Van Dyke Brown	2 minutes full sun.	brown/blackish-brown/white	Paper Organic fabric	WARNING: Silver Nitrate is very dangerous.
Inkodye	10 minutes full sun.	all	Paper Organic fabric	unknown
Rockland Emulsion	enlarger light	b-w (can be toned)	Paper, stone, ceramic, wood, sized cloth.	-----
Photo Aluminum	enlarger light	b-w (can be toned)	-----	-----
Photo Linen	enlarger	b-w (can be toned)	-----	-----
Screen Print	4-8 minutes full sun	all	All flat surfaces: glass, plexiglass, fabric, paper, wood ceramics, tile.	Bichromate in direct emulsions. Use ventilation while printing.
B&W Xerox	-----	Black/White	All papers. Transfer to fabric.	-----
Color Xerox/3M	-----	all	All papers. Acetate Transfer to fabric.	-----
Magazine Rubbing	-----	all	All papers. Smooth fabric.	Use ventilation.

Advantages	Disadvantages	Permanence on paper	Permanence on fabric
Premixed, economical fast, perfect registration. Two year shelf life.	Transparent colors need several coats to achieve density	Excellent	Machine washable
Painterly qualities, economical.	Slow & temperamental Must be homemade.	Excellent	Not washable.
Economical for large areas.	Color limitations. Needs a very strong light source.	Excellent	Not washable
Beautiful continuous tone print quality. Very light sensitive.	Difficult to coat without staining surface & your hands. Expensive (Silver Nitrate is $8-14/ounce)	Excellent	Not washable
A bright dye for fabric that leaves no stiffness.	Should only be photo-screened.	Unknown	Permanent if used according to directions.
Because it's sensitive to projected negatives it's good for 3 dimensional objects.	Delicate emulsion... takes skill to coat and process.	Moderate	Not washable
Easy to use	Expensive	Excellent	-----
Easy to use	An imported product not readily available.	-----	Hand wash
Best way to do multiple prints.	Extensive preparation not recommended unless you plan to do multiples.	Excellent	Washable, depending on ink used and material screened.
Quick image without a darkroom	Black and white only.	Depends on the paper	Not washable
Quick image without a darkroom	Expensive and not readily available.	Unknown	Not washable
Quick image without a darkroom.	Only 1 rubbing per image. Image is reversed.	Excellent	Not washable

HELPFUL PRODUCTS

Unless otherwise noted, most of these products can be found at graphic art supply stores and some photography stores.

FILM OPAQUE—This chalky red or black "paint" can be applied to your negatives with a brush or pen. The areas blocked out will not print. If you wish, you can remove opaque with water. Opaque can be applied to acetate, spattered, scratched through, etc., for special effects.

GOLDENROD—Also called "masking sheets," this opaque yellow or orange paper is available in plain or ruled sheets. It is used in offset printing for the masking of negatives and type into "flats" to be placed on offset plates and exposed through. The sheets are translucent when placed on a light table, so windows for negatives are easily cut and the negatives are taped in place.

Goldenrod is very useful for masking or "stripping" your negatives in all light sensitive processes.

BLACK PHOTOGRAPHIC TAPE—This masking tape is available at photo stores. It is helpful in the construction of pinhole cameras.

RED CELLOPHANE TAPE—This red transparent tape is used in "stripping" masked sheets for offset printing. The tape blocks out light and can be used on ortho negatives or plain acetate to mask straight lines or to piece negatives together.

PRESS TYPE and **TEXTURE SCREENS**—Sheets of type or printed textures (like fake bricks, dots, stars) can be used to create interesting stencil materials for light sensitive processes.

SEAL FUSION 4000—An archival, removable, self trimming dry mount adhesive suitable for mounting a variety of products including paper of all types, fabric, and color prints.

CONTACT FRAME—Premier makes standard 4x5, 8x10, 11x14 and 16x20 wooden frames with glass which hold surfaces in tight contact during exposure. Watch flea markets for second hand contact frames.

MAGNIFYING LENS or **LINEN TESTER**—These magnifying lenses come in little folding metal stands and are available at graphic arts supplies. You need one to inspect halftones and pinholes for pinhole cameras.

QUARTZ LIGHT UNIT—These small light units are available at photography stores. They are relatively inexpensive and the bulbs are replaceable. This is an excellent light source because the bulbs give consistent light until they burn out.

PRESSURIZED SPRAY CAN—These are available at hardware stores. They are small spray can units that fit on top of glass containers which you can fill with any fine liquid that you wish to spray.

FABRIC MARKING PENS—These ball-point embroidery pens are filled with dye and can be used for hand coloring fabric pieces. They can be found in hobby stores.

HELPFUL READING

Some of these books contain extensive written material. Others contain good reproductions of work in a variety of processes. Some of the titles may be out of print, so you will need to look for them in a library. Unless otherwise noted, most of them are available by mail from Light Impressions Corporation, Box 3012, Rochester, N.Y. 14614.

CHRONOLOGY OF PHOTOGRAPHY—*Arnold Gassan* (out of print)
Includes a discussion of mixed media and non-silver work of the 70's.

CONTEMPORARY TRENDS—*Howard Kaplan, ed.* Columbia College, 1976.
Work reproduced includes images by Robert Heinecken and Todd Walker.

DARKROOM—*Eleanor Lewis, ed.* Lustrum Press
The chapter by Betty Hahn on gum bichromate printing will answer most of your questions. She describes its use on fabric and includes a bibliography.

FRONTIERS OF PHOTOGRAPHY—*Time-Life Series*
Some contemporary work reproduced in color, notably Catherine Jansen's blue print bedroom.

A HANDBOOK FOR CONTEMPORARY PHOTOGRAPHY—
Arnold Gassan, 4th Edition, 1977.
An excellent text covering a wide range of processes including gum printing, cyanotype, silkscreen, photogravure, Kwik Print and others.

THE HOLE THING: A Manual of PinHole Fotografy—*Jim Shull*
A clearly written booklet on pinhole photography.

3M COLOR—*Friends of Photography, 1973* (350 copies).
Beautiful booklet contains original prints produced on the 3M Color-in-Color machine as well as several articles about this machine.

MODERN HELIOGRAPHIC PROCESSES
A reprint of an 1888 text including cyanotype, calotype, carbon print, and gum print formulas. An advanced source of information. Some of the chemistry is very hard to locate today.

NON SILVER PRINTING PROCESSES—*Peter Bunnell, ed.,* 1973.
A reprint of 4 essays dealing technically with photogravure, gum printing, oil and bromoil and platinotype.

THE PHOTOGRAPHY CATALOG—Norman Snyder, Harper & Row, 1976
Chapter 14 on Unique Processes is somewhat sketchy, but shows some work by artists using these processes.

PHOTOGRAPHY WITHOUT A CAMERA—*Patra Holter* 1972
How to make photographs with a minimum of equipment. A discussion of photograms, sun prints, and painting with developers and toners. A well illustrated and carefully researched book.

PHOTOGRAVURE HANDBOOK—*Samuel Rothberg,*   Rye Press, 1976.
An informative 41 page description of this process.

PHOTO SYNTHESIS—   Cornell University, 1976.
Black and white reproductions of work by 57 artists in mixed photo media.

SOME ASPECTS OF AMERICAN PHOTOGRAPHY, 1976—
                              University of Missouri-St. Louis.

Beautifully produced show catalog with reproductions and commentary on
the work of 19 photographers. Good color reproduction of a Betty Hahn fabric
piece and a toned photograph by Benno Friedman

UNTITLED #11: EMERGING LOS ANGELES PHOTOGRAPHERS—
                              Friends of Photography
A well produced survey of new work including 13 color reproductions.

KODAK PUBLICATIONS:

CREATIVE DARKROOM TECHNIQUES—   1973
Includes information and reproductions of gum prints, photo silkscreens,
among other nonsilver processes.

A SENSITIZER FOR PAPER, CLOTH AND SIMILAR FABRICS

Pamphlet # AJ-5   Technical formulas for 2 types of brown prints.

KODAK AUTOSCREEN ORTHO FILM: HOW IT WORKS   Pamphlet # P-21
15 page descriptive on the use of Autoscreen film.

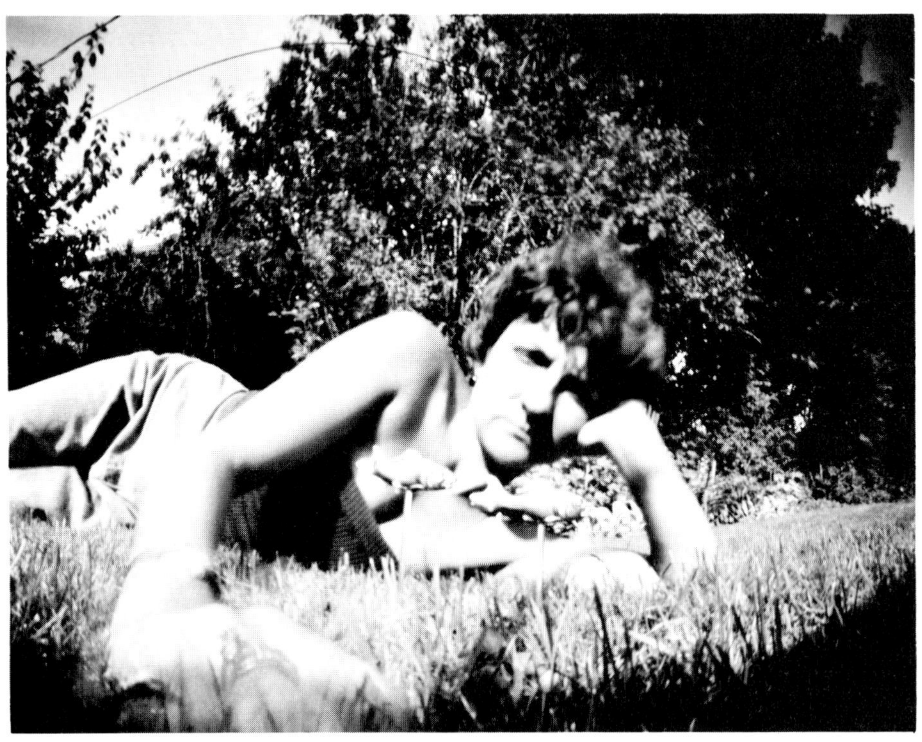

This 4 x 5 Autoscreen image was made with a grits pinhole camera.

Visual Studies Workshop
Rochester, N.Y.

FINE LINE DEVELOPER—*Tim Hearsum*   1975
Explains in detail the use of Fine Line Developer to achieve random dot images
for use in photoscreen printing.

IMAGING WITH LIGHT SENSITIVE MATERIALS—*Deborah Flynn*   1976
Cyanotype, Van Dyke Brown, Gum Bichromate and Casein printing presented
in a beautifully printed 12 page booklet.

PHOTOGRAPHIC SLIDE SETS

These sets were produced from the original artwork and are distributed by
Light Impressions Corporation. Write for a recent slide catalog, or look for
these sets in university slide collections.

DARRYL CURRAN	Van Dyke Brown prints with added color.
PETER DELORY	Recent hand toned black and white photographs.
ROBERT FICHTER	Blue and brown prints on paper with drawing.
BETTY HAHN	Gum prints on paper and fabric.
SYL LABROT	Dye transfer, photoscreen prints and random dot images from Pleasure Beach.
BEA NETTLES	An assortment of mixed media work including Rockland Emulsion on fabric, hand toned photographs, gum prints, photo linen, magazine rubbing and other processes.
BEA NETTLES	Recent set includes only Kwik Print images.
SONIA SHERIDAN	Work in several techniques by the founder of the Generative Systems program at the Chicago Art Institute.
TODD WALKER	Recent work in offset lithography and silkscreen.
JOHN WOOD	Printmaking and photographic combinations.
60's CONTINUUM	Work by several artists in a variety of approaches. This set documents a major show held at the International Museum of Photography at George Eastman House in 1972.

SAFETY TIPS

Check the comparison chart for specific hazards of each process. Careless use of any of the processes could have serious cumulative effects.

CARE IN THE USE OF EMULSIONS
Always wash your hands after coating emulsions. Better yet, wear plastic gloves.

Don't eat food in your studio.

During the first washout of emulsion, keep your hands out of the wash water. This is when most of the unexposed chemicals flow off.

BICHROMATE POISONING: An itching, blistering of the skin caused in some people by extensive exposure to bichromate (in gum printing, Kwik Print, silkscreen direct emulsions)

SILVER NITRATE BURNS: Contact with Van Dyke Brown print solution will cause brown stains which will not wash off the skin. More serious is contact with concentrated Silver Nitrate which forms black silver deposits under the skin. Silver Nitrate in either form is dangerous because it is absorbed by the body through the skin.

CARE IN THE DARKROOM
Some people are quite sensitive to Kodalith A B Developer. It can cause their hands to blister and swell. Wear gloves or use tongs if you are prone to such things. At the very least, wash your hands often. As with other chemicals in a closed space, it would be wise to use an exhaust fan for adequate ventilation.

CARE WITH THE USE OF SOLVENTS
Always use ventilation when working with solvents, especially when screen printing or doing magazine rubbings.

CARE WITH YOUR LIGHT SOURCE
High levels of ultraviolet light are not good for your eyes. **Never** look directly into a carbon arc lamp or any other strong light source. To do so could burn tissues in your eyes.

Carbon arc lamps produce ozone as they burn. They must be vented with a powerful fan while in use, or the fumes can make you quite sick.

OTHER BRIGHT IDEAS

SIMPLE DRYING BOX FOR COATED PAPER AND FABRIC

Find a large flat cardboard box; the type offset printing paper is shipped in is great. Cut a hole in the top and insert a hair drier hose in it. Coated materials may be tacked inside the box with push pins and dried in total darkness. A good option is to paint the inside of the box with polyurethane so that it is moisture proof and washable with a damp sponge.

BUY PLASTIC CLOTHESPINS AND LINE

When you hang coated emulsion pieces to dry, chemicals often get trapped in wooden pins causing stains on the next piece. Plastic clothespins can be rinsed off periodically. A plastic or aluminum wire clothesline is suggested because it will not absorb chemicals either.

GOT SOME OLD STORM WINDOWS?

These make good exposure units for large pieces because the frame around a storm window adds needed weight and gives good contact.

Storm windows also have the sharp edges of the glass contained and are less likely to break than single ply glass.

They can also be made into makeshift light tables. Back the glass with tracing paper or frosted contact paper. Set the backed glass over a box in which you have installed some sort of lighting fixture. The light will be diffused somewhat by the paper. Be sure the bulb is far enough away from the paper surface so there is no heat buildup.

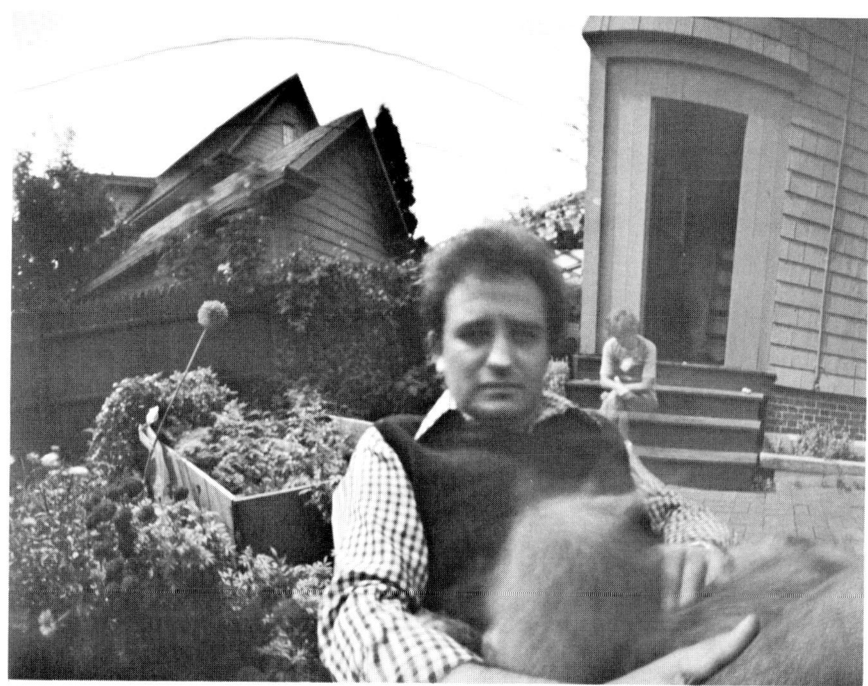

This 4 x 5 Autoscreen image was made with a grits pinhole camera.

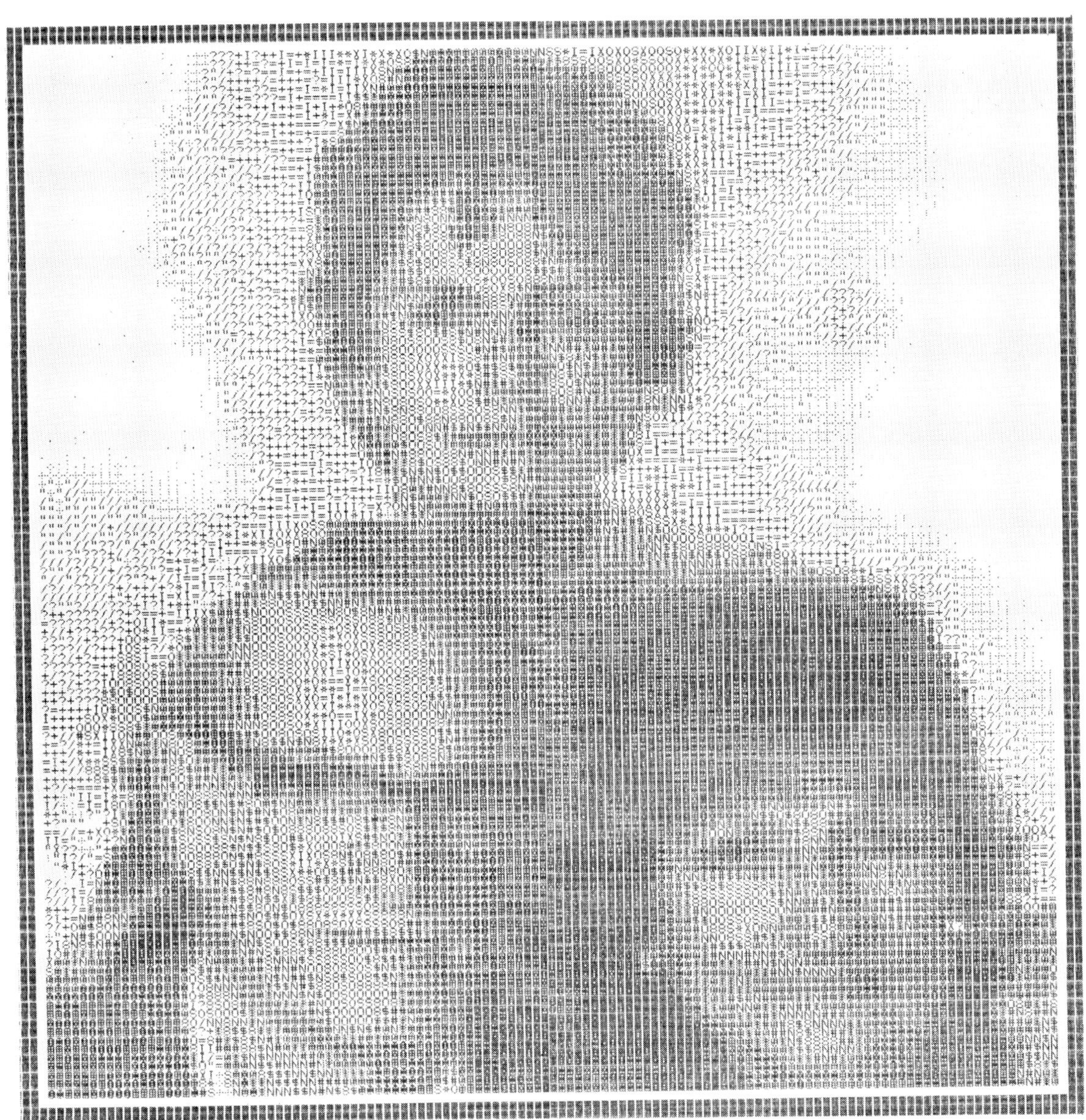

Computer Portrait of Victor, Grace and Bea Nettles. April 1977.

A note on the illustrations: All images in the book are by Bea Nettles except the family snapshot on page 9 which was taken by Victor Nettles in the early 50's.